"So we preach . . ."

D1634414

"So we preach . . ."

SERMONS BY MINISTERS OF THE FREE CHURCH OF SCOTLAND

EDITED BY
WILLIAM D. GRAHAM

KNOX PRESS (EDINBURGH)
15 NORTH BANK STREET
EDINBURGH EH1 2LS
1976

Printed in Great Britain by
Robert MacLehose & Company Limited
Printers to the University of Glasgow

Contents

Preface

This present volume of sermons by ministers of the Free Church of Scotland bears testimony to the high place which preaching occupies in the total ministry of our Church.

Holding, as we do, the view that the Scriptures are indeed the Word of God, divinely inspired and inerrant, we regard the preaching of the Word as of the utmost importance.

The ministers who have contributed to this volume are worthy representatives of our ministry and, while their style of preaching varies and the presentation of the message differs from person to person, the essential content of the preaching does not vary. Each one seeks to present the Truth as it is contained in the Holy Scriptures, for only as we do this will our preaching have that authority from God which makes it effective.

For the purposes of editorial uniformity some slight alterations have been made to the format of some of the Sermons, but the essential individuality of each has been maintained.

May the blessing of the Lord accompany the reading of these sermons as they now enjoy the privilege of a wider "congregation" than when they were first delivered.

WILLIAM D. GRAHAM

Edinburgh

PARTNERSHIP IN SERVICE

"Workers together with Him."
2 COR. 6:1

From Paul's many allusions to the Christian ministry it is evident that he regards it as of all occupations the most exalted. He may speak of himself as "less than the least of all saints", "the least of the apostles" and "not meet to be called an apostle", but, invariably, he magnifies his office. The Christian minister, he declares, is an ambassador for Christ, a plenipotentiary of heaven, engaged in the service of the kingdom which lies nearest the King's heart, the salvation of men. He had not been a follower of Christ during our Lord's earthly ministry, and consequently was not a member of the little group to whom Jesus gave the great commission, to go into all the world and preach the gospel to every creature. But he had received his marching orders from Christ as directly as they had. On the Damascus Road the life-transforming encounter had taken place, and the former persecutor had gladly fallen in with his new Master's purpose for him, to bear his name before the Gentiles, and kings, and the children of Israel. All the shining gifts, all the burning zeal, all the surging energy that had formerly marked the fanatical persecutor were now transferred and consecrated to the service of Christ. And the late-comer to the goodly company of the Apostles was just as keenly aware as any of his brethren were of the accompanying presence, in all his service, of the Master Who in the great commission had said, "And lo I am with you alway".

The erstwhile persecutor was now a "worker together with Him".

Let us note from these words:

(1) The position occupied

"Workers together *with Him*." For He was no idle Master. It was as a worker that the Son of God Himself appeared among men, and in this, as in every other aspect of His character, He is the perfect example. His devotion was absolute. "My meat," He said, "is to do the will of Him that sent Me, and to finish His work". And again, "I must work the works of Him that sent Me, while it is day: the night cometh when no man can work". The work was arduous. "If Adam has not sinned," says Matthew Henry, "he had not sweated." It was hard work winning his daily bread from the ground that was under a curse because of his sin; but if the sweat of his brow was the measure of his toil who can estimate the travail that is marked in the sweat of the Second Adam which, in Gethsemane, was as great drops of blood falling to the ground? Surely this supreme example of self-sacrificing service rebukes our self-regarding slackness.

> Lord, when I am weary with toiling,
> And burdensome seem Thy commands,
> If my load should lead to complaining,
> Lord, show me Thy hands—
> Thy nail-pierced hands, Thy cross-torn hands,
> My Saviour, show me Thy hands.
>
> Christ, if my footsteps should falter
> And I be prepared for retreat.
> If desert or thorn cause lamenting,
> Lord, show me Thy feet—
> Thy bleeding feet, Thy nail-scarred feet,
> My Saviour show me Thy feet.
>
> O God, dare I show Thee
> *My* hands and *my* feet?

It was as a worker rejoicing at the completion of His work that He cried from the Cross; "It is finished". It was an echo of what He had previously said in His High Priestly prayer, "I have glorified Thee on the earth; I have finished the work which Thou gavest me to do". "Only once," writes F. W. Boreham, "in the world's history did a finishing touch bring a work to absolute perfection; and on that day of days a single flaw would have shattered the hope of the ages."

We sometimes hear it said as preachers press upon their hearers their obligation to serve the Lord, "God has no hands to work with but our hands. He has no lips to proclaim His message but our lips. He has no feet to carry the good news to other lands but our feet." But, however good the intention that lies behind the words, they simply are not true; and they limit the Holy One of Israel. The fiat of Eternal Sovereignty alone was enough to bring all things into being in the creation of the universe; and in the execution of the work of Redemption it was a solitary figure that trod the wine-press. He did it alone, and of the people there was none with Him.

And yet it pleased Him in extending His kingdom in the world to call His redeemed to become "workers together with Him". He knew the joy and satisfaction of a congenial task, and He desired His people to share it with Him. The call of the Gospel thus combines emancipation and consecration. It promises rest, not in indolence but in service. If it removes one yoke it imposes another. The slaves of sin become servants of righteousness. Constraint is indeed. exercised in the recruitment, but it is the conscription of love. For it is in the immediate context of the words we are considering that Paul tells how he came into the service of Christ. "For the love of Christ constraineth us," he writes, "because we thus judge, that if one died for all, then were all dead; and that He died for all, that they which live should not henceforth live unto themselves, but unto Him which died for them, and rose again."

It was a constraint joyfully yielded to. It was the surrender of the now liberated will and the conquered heart. It issued from a true knowledge of God in Christ, and an experience of His saving grace. "Who art Thou, Lord?" the humbled persecutor had cried when he came under the arrest of love. And when the desired identification was made the surrender followed; "Lord, what wilt Thou have me to do?" Under a sense of undischargeable obligation he gave

3

himself without reserve to the service of his new Master.

> Make me a captive Lord, and then I shall be free;
> Force me to render up my sword and I shall conqueror be.
> My will is not my own till Thou hast made it Thine.
> If it would reach the monarch's throne, it must its crown resign.

"Workers together with Him"; what surprising choices the Lord often makes in calling men into His service. And all the more surprising because they are not made under the pressures of need. When our nation was building up its armed forces at the beginning of the Second World War many who in normal times would have been judged substandard for national service were called to the help of the Crown in a time of peril and unpreparedness. The situation of extreme urgency which had so suddenly arisen required that all available manpower should be mustered. Normal standards must be lowered, at least until the war-machine was fully operative.

But there was no straining of God's resources when He called men into the warfare of His Kingdom. And it was not because no others were available to Him that He gathered into His armies the foolish things of the world, the weak things of the world, the base and despised things of the world, but because the weakness of men was His chosen medium for the displaying of the perfection of His power. The treasure was committed to earthen vessels that the excellency of the power might be seen to be of God and not of men, to the end that no flesh should glory in His presence.

Yet it looked as if His cause were doomed from the outset. "Have any of the rulers or of the Pharisees believed on Him?" scoffed the religious leaders. Under such patronage, and with such recognition His cause might indeed prosper. But ignorant and unlearned men, people of the peasant stock, fishermen of Galilee, what possible influence could *they* exert? By worldly standards the Pharisees were right when they measured the workers against the work. And Gamaliel was right when, having made his measurement he said, ". . . if this counsel or this work be of men, it will come to nought". It was all a confirmation of what the Master Himself had said, ". . . without Me ye can do nothing".

4

But this brings us secondly to:

(2) The power promised

For who will doubt that there is an assurance of empowerment implied in this description of the Lord's servants as "workers together with Him"? The promise is made explicit in the parting words of Christ to His disciples on the Mount of Olives. "Ye shall receive power after that the Holy Ghost is come upon you"; and in that power they were to be witnesses unto Him, "both in Jerusalem, and in all Judea, and in Samaria, and unto the uttermost part of the earth". But they must "tarry in Jerusalem", until they were "endued with power from on high". "Workers together with Him"—break that partnership for a moment; measure those early disciples against the tasks assigned them, and how pitifully inadequate they seem! A mere Gideon's band against a confederate army which was as grasshoppers for multitude . . . and as the sand by the seaside which cannot be numbered. But at the battle-cry of that feeble army, "The sword of the Lord and of Gideon", the Lord set every man's sword against his fellow in the camp of the enemy, "and all the host ran, and cried, and fled".

In the same empowering alliance the stripling David counter-challenged the champion of the Philistines "in the name of the Lord of hosts, the God of the armies of Israel" whom he had defied; and his trust was honoured with resounding victory. Samson, weak as other men, when the Lord departed from him, regained his great strength in answer to prayer and broke the power of Israel's enemy. "Workers together with God!" Moses saw how that alliance would work out in Israel's future, and with prophetic tongue exclaimed, "Happy art thou, O Israel, who is like unto thee, O people saved by the Lord, the shield of thy help, and Who is the sword of thy excellency, and thine enemies shall be found liars unto thee; and thou shalt tread upon their high places".

And Israel's Psalmist, in later years, reviewing the long list of Israel's triumphs over the centuries, gives the glory of them all to Israel's God. "If it had not been the Lord who was on our side, now may Israel say; if it had not been the

Lord who was on our side, when men rose up against us; then the waters had overwhelmed us, the stream had gone over our soul. . . . Our help is in the name of the Lord, who made heaven and earth."

Israel's sword was indeed active in these conflicts; but "they got not the land in possession by their own sword, neither did their own arm save them; but Thy right hand, and thine arm, and the light of thy countenance, because thou hadst a favour unto them".

And there we have the pattern of the Church's warfare today. It is not without significance that she is compared to an army, and that her activities in the world are compared to a warfare. She is an aggregate of individuals called and commissioned to press the claims of Christ upon a disaffected world, prosecuting the campaign in His way, waging the warfare in His strength, trusting for victory to His promise.

"If this work be of men," said Gamaliel, "it will come to nought. But if it be of God, ye cannot overthrow it." And that it *was* of God the apostles themselves were always quick to testify. "Ye men of Israel," said Peter to the people who came together to see the man who had been healed at the Beautiful Gate of the Temple, "why marvel ye at this? or why look ye so earnestly on us, as though by our own power or holiness we had made this man to walk? The God of Abraham, and of Isaac, and of Jacob, the God of our fathers hath glorified His Son Jesus . . . and His name, through faith in His name, hath made this man strong, whom ye see and know. . . ." And when at Lystra the people cried, "the gods are come down to us in the likeness of men" because of the miracle of healing which they witnessed there, the disciples disclaimed all credit for the wonder which had been wrought, ascribing the glory of it all to the power of God which had wrought through them. "Who is Paul" wrote this apostle to the quarrelling factions at Corinth, "and who is Apollos, but ministers by whom ye believed, even as the Lord gave to every man. I have planted, Apollos watered; but God gave the increase. So then neither is he that planteth any thing, neither he that watereth; but God that giveth the increase." If in another

6

epistle he appears to us to change his testimony, is it because we have stopped reading too soon. For if he claims, "I can do all things" this ability, he immediately adds, is "through Christ which strengtheneth me". It is thus that the "worm Jacob" is made a "new sharp threshing instrument having teeth"; and is enabled to "thresh the mountains, and beat them small, and . . . make the hills as chaff".

But let us look finally at:

(3) The prospect cherished

From the nature of the partnership described in our text it is evident that failure is completely ruled out and success ensured. There are other passages of Scripture from the pen of this great Apostle which reveal the strength of his confidence that the cause to which he had consecrated his life would reach fulfilment in spite of the relentless opposition of enemies and notwithstanding the apathy and lethargy of many who profess to be its friends. "Let us not be weary in well doing:" he urges the Galatians, "for in due season we shall reap if we faint not." He exhorts the Corinthians in similar strain; "be ye steadfast, unmovable, always abounding in the work of the Lord, forasmuch as ye know that your labour is not in vain in the Lord". Reverses there were, but his faith remained constant. From a prison cell, knowing that he was "about to be offered" and that the "time of his departure was at hand", he expresses to his son in the faith, Timothy, his confident expectation of ultimate victory. "I have fought a good fight, I have finished my course, I have kept the faith. Henceforth there is laid up for me a crown of righteousness, which the Lord, the righteous judge, shall give me at that day; and not to me only, but unto all them also that love His appearing." There is a cynical view of faith which defines it as "believing that which you know to be untrue", but cynical definitions are notoriously untrustworthy. Faith, according to a truer definition, is "the substance of things hoped for, the evidence of things not seen". And Christian faith has always something trustworthy to cling to, even the sure promises of a covenant-keeping God. Trials of faith there will be; times when there is no awareness of the Divine yoke-fellow's Presence; times

7

such as the disciples passed through when they battled against contrary winds on the Sea of Galilee, "And it was now dark, and Jesus was not come to them". But His eye was upon them in all their toil and terror; and at the right moment He joined them saying reassuringly, "It is I; be not afraid".

If they cast Paul into prison at Philippi, the result, for him, was a fuller awareness of the Master's Presence; for that, surely, must be the secret of the song at midnight which the prisoners heard issuing from the inner prison. If the situation became menacing at Corinth, it brought him that word of comfort and command, "Be not afraid, but speak, and hold not thy peace. For I am with thee, and no man shall set on thee to hurt thee: for I have much people in this city." When the tempest broke upon the ship that was bearing him to Rome, and all hope of deliverance was abandoned, it was Paul who became the rallying centre of the despairing ship's company, saying, "I exhort you to be of good cheer; for there shall be no loss of any man's life among you, but of the ship. For there stood by me this night the angel of God, Whose I am and Whom I serve, saying, "Fear not, Paul: thou must be brought before Caesar; and, lo, God hath given thee all them that sail with thee . . .". If friends failed him at a critical hour in Rome, the effect was the deepening of his trust in his unfailing partner. "No man stood with me," he records, "but all men forsook me. . . . Nothwithstanding, the Lord stood with me, and strengthened me." Scourged, beaten, stoned, imprisoned, constantly confronted by danger and the threat of a violent death, he nevertheless retains all his confidence in the righteousness and ultimate triumph of the cause to which he had dedicated his life. "Now thanks be unto God," he writes, "which always causeth us to triumph in Christ. . . ." The taste of victory was upon the very trials which led to it! "Our light affliction which is but for a moment worketh for us a far more exceeding and eternal weight of glory."

Sir Robert Stopworth, who commanded one of the ships with which Nelson dispersed and defeated an enemy fleet far greater than his own, wrote at the very height of the sore struggle which preceded the victory, "We are half starved, and otherwise inconvenienced by being so long out of port. But our reward is—*we are with Nelson.*"

To be a worker together with such a Commander was assurance and compensation enough for all the hardship involved. That Commander died in the hour of his greatest victory. He was given an honoured grave among the most famous of his countrymen; but the fame attaching to his name, despite the many memorials erected by a grateful nation to perpetuate it, was of a fading order; and little remained to the men who had served and suffered with him but their memories, their battle-scars and the pittances allowed by the nation for their sustenance in declining years.

The fellow workers of Christ fare differently. The Captain of their salvation died indeed in the hour of glorious triumph. But He rose again. He ascended to the right hand of eternal majesty, and from that seat of power He directs the warfare of His Kingdom, sending no man on a warfare at his own charges, but supplying the needs of all who rally to His standard until His sovereignty is universally acknowledged and His enemies are made His footstool. And the claim which He presents in the interests of all who are "workers together with Him" shall be fully met; "Father, I will that they also whom Thou has given Me be with Me where I am; that they may behold My glory which Thou hast given me; for Thou lovedst Me before the foundation of the world".

To speak of our Lord's death upon the Cross—as some irreverently do—as "a splendid gamble" is really to charge Him with the imprudence of the king in His own parable who, failing to count the cost, marched with his 10,000 men against another king who completely outmatched him. Christ knew the cost of victory from all eternity and knew also that He was well able to meet it. The song of victory was composed before ever the battle was joined. More lasting His fame than that of any other victor, and more abundant the rewards of those who serve under His standard than those of the men who subject themselves to other dominions.

> His name for ever shall endure,
> Last like the sun it shall:
> Men shall be bless'd in Him, and bless'd
> All nations shall Him call.

But as "workers together with Him" let us ever bear in mind that we serve under His direction. Obedience is the condition of power, and the only power by which the Church can fulfil its purpose in the world is the power which energised her at the beginning—the power of Pentecost. She may improve her organisation, modernise her methods, increase her wealth, perfect her planning, bring to her task all that social influence and material resources can contribute but she will stand discredited and helpless in the presence of a resurgent paganism if she departs from her marching orders. For the weapons of this warfare are not carnal. The energy of the flesh cannot do the work of the Spirit. The sufficiency of the Church is not of men but of God, and the communication of that sufficiency cannot be expected where His will is resisted, His command ignored.

The miracle at Cana of Galilee was made to depend on the obedience of the servants who in a golden hour became workers together with Him. "Whatsoever He saith unto you, do it" was then and is now the rule of Christian service. Reason may at times wish to sit in judgment on His ways, and even presume to amend His orders. There seemed to be little point in carrying water into a festal chamber where the company were waiting for wine. There appeared to be no purpose in casting a net on the right side of the ship after having toiled all the night long and taken nothing. To anoint the eyes of a blind man with clay and then bid him go and wash himself at the pool of Siloam might be judged a mockery of his misery. To send men into all the world with the Gospel of the Cross was to cast a stumbling block in the way of the Jew, to provoke the ridicule of the Gentile, and to invite utter failure, except for one thing; that in every case the bidding came from the Christ who in issuing it said, "All power in heaven and in earth is given unto Me . . . and lo, I am with you alway, even to the end of the age".

And as the workers receive their discharge it will be

with His commendation, and His eternal reward; "Well done, good and faithful servant, enter thou into the joy of thy Lord". Joined with Him in service, they will also be joined with Him in glory. For if we suffer with Him we shall also reign with Him. For He is faithful Who said, "To him that overcometh will I grant to sit with Me in My throne, even as I also overcame, and am set down with My Father in His throne".

G. N. M. Collins

CHRIST AS HIGH PRIEST

". . . an high priest for ever . . ."
HEB. 6:20

A visitor to a magnificent building, such as a French Gothic Cathedral, will form a better impression of the grandeur of the whole design if he views the exterior and interior from several angles. The grand subject of the Bible is Christ. It is a many-sided and inexhaustible theme but the inspired writers enable us to look at it in a variety of helpful ways. The special contribution of the Epistle to the Hebrews is to focus attention on Christ's priestly service. Some other Biblical books mention or imply His priesthood but nowhere else is it so fully or instructively explained. Let us consider *four* aspects of it.

(1) The purpose of His priesthood

In this age of unparalleled progress in many directions, few things are more evident than the marked absence of a general improvement in social morality. Of course, certain misguided people hail the abandonment of an absolute moral standard in favour of some type of situational ethics, or permissiveness, as clear proof of notable progress. But such an attitude is at variance with God's Word and the testimony of history. The prevalence of dishonesty, robbery, murder, sexual offences and broken marriages leaves little room for doubt that a large proportion of modern society is not much better in this respect than the society of the New Testament world. And the New Testament mentions these same evils among sins resulting from the broken harmony in man's relation to God. It attributes the persistence of sin with all the distress it causes in this life, and the appalling penalty appointed for the unforgiven hereafter to man's revolt against divine authority. To be sure, sin is not confined to those convicted of gross moral offences in criminal courts. Their wrong-doing is symptomatic of the sin that is in every man's heart, though manifesting its presence in different ways and degrees. The Bible teaches clearly that all have sinned, and each man's greatest need is reconciliation to God. And this is no less true today than when the Gospel first made known the way of reconciliation. Human ingenuity could not devise a way nor could human resources provide it. But God in His love and wisdom has done both. To reconcile God and men is the great object of Christ's priesthood, and through it God offers a way whereby the penitent can be forgiven and welcomed to the fellowship and service of His believing family.

(2) His qualifications for office

To begin with *He is God's choice*. Scripture declares repeatedly that God Himself appointed Christ High Priest. This fact is of no small importance. According to the proverb, "Fools make a mock at sin". They make light of guilt. But sin is an evil of incalculable potential. Notwithstanding all the light the Bible sheds upon it, insoluble mystery still surrounds its origin, the greatness of its offence to God and the extent of the ruin to which it renders the guilty liable. God alone understands sin's sinister nature and alienating power. But when He, who clearly grasps every aspect of man's plight as a sinner, took the initiative in reconciliation, determined the method and chose the person to undertake the work, He laid a firm foundation for human hope.

But again *He is God's Son*. And beyond question His sonship is altogether unique. Adam as created in God's image was His son. But sin made him an unworthy and banished son. Hosea calls Israel God's son. The nation became so by adoption when God rescued them from Egypt and made a covenant with them. Among their best representatives were Moses and the faithful prophets, yet Christ stands in a relation to God which even they do not share. Believers in Christ are granted the status of sons of God but Christ alone is called the only begotten son. Angels are sometimes called sons of God but they are commanded to worship Christ. Nor is this all. He Himself is God, possessing fully His Father's nature, character and power. Moreover His divine sonship gives Him an unlimited and intimate knowledge of the Father. He shares both His knowledge of sin and His loving desire that sinners should be reconciled to Him by His Son's priesthood.

Further *He had a sinless human career*. To accomplish His Father's purpose He became His servant in human nature. By His birth at Bethlehem He took man's nature with all its essential limitations into union with His divine nature. As man "He learned obedience by the things which he suffered." In boyhood, at the carpenter's bench, and in years of public ministry He felt the power of temptation. He encountered growing opposition from the envious and the prejudiced. He was unjustly condemned and crucified. He endured sharp physical pain, keen mental distress and deep spiritual suffering before He died. Thus He discovered by personal experience the costliness of obedience that involves suffering and, in His case, unfathomable suffering. But He committed no sin. His supernatural birth prevented the sin that is present in all members of a fallen race from passing to Him. In no circumstances did He yield to temptation. When He challenged His opponents to accuse Him of sin they were silent, and the accusations made, at other times, by His enemies were baseless. Nevertheless by His manifold encounters with temptation He acquired rich human sympathy with the harassed and tempted who come to Him for support and deliverance.

Once more *He has an endless life*. As God He is immortal. As man He died, but only in the voluntary discharge of His supreme priestly duty, which was to offer Himself as a once-for-all sacrifice for the ungodly. Let Himself explain the surrender of His life. "No man," He said, "taketh it from me, but I lay it down of myself. I have power to lay it down, and I have power to take it again. This commandment have I received of my Father" (John 10:18). Accordingly He rose from the grave on the third day never again to die. And He evermore possesses in heaven in union with His divine nature the human nature in which He triumphed over temptation, suffering and death.

(3) The once-for-all sacrifice He offered

"Hebrews" strongly emphasises that Christ obtained salvation for those He represented by a single sacrifice. And we are not left in doubt as to the sacrifice meant. *It was not intercession alone.* The Epistle of James assures us that "The effectual, fervent prayer of a righteous man availeth much" (Jas. 5:16). And no more righteous man than the sinless Christ ever offered intercessory prayers to God on earth. But apart from another offering, not even His prayers could benefit Peter, future believers, or His enemies for whom He asked mercy and grace. *It was not the sacrifice of a good life*, devoted to loving service for others. The final chapter of "Hebrews" mentions *doing good* as a sacrifice with which God is well-pleased. Christ went about doing good in Palestine. Never before was the compassionate loving kindness of God so perfectly revealed as when He preached the Gospel to the poor, healed men's bodies, liberated their spirits, wept at their sorrow and brought their dead to life. He has indeed left us a challenging and searching example of doing good. He desires us to share its spirit. Yet neither His example nor any imitation of it can reconcile us to God. *It was not the sacrifice involved in martyrdom.* Christ spoke of Himself as a prophet. He claimed that He came into the world to bear witness to the truth. Once when referring to His death He said, "It cannot be that a prophet perish out of Jerusalem" (Luke 13:33). And in that city He was condemned by the Sanhedrin because He remained loyal to the truth He had declared. A martyr prophet, sealing with blood an incomparable body of teaching! From one point of view He certainly was. But neither the authoritative teaching nor the martyr-death, nor both together sufficed to save a single individual.

It was in anticipation of a death far more terrible than martyrdom that the courageous Christ prayed with strong crying, accompanied by tears and bloody sweat, in Gethsemane. What He saw ahead of Him was the guilt of the people He represented being reckoned as His guilt and He Himself being dealt with by God as guilty instead of them. It was in willing submission to this dread experience that, to quote "Hebrews", "through the eternal spirit". He offered Himself without spot to God (5:14). The eternal spirit has been understood to mean the Holy Spirit who sustained His human nature. We do not question that the Spirit, in whose power His ministry was carried out, assisted Him in the culminating act of His mission. At the same time the words underlying the translation may point rather to His divine nature. Though itself incapable of death, it was united to the human life He laid down and gave infinite merit to His offering.

This was the once-for-all sacrifice God required and it was offered at Calvary. There criminals, suffering for their misdeeds, hung on either side of the Son of God. There criminals stood before Him, guilty of His unjust death. There abuse was heaped upon Him. There, at length, He uttered the cry of dereliction that told of distress far deeper than that of body or mind. But there too rang out His triumphant announcement, "It is finished", (John 19:30) anticipating the close of His priestly work on earth. For at Calvary, contrary to the intentions of wicked men and entirely unknown to them, God had been at work in holy love providing a way of reconciliation by the substitutionary sacrifice of His beloved Son. Christ's resurrection is proof that His sacrifice is accepted. At His ascension He began the second part of His priestly work which consists of heavenly intercession. He engages in this work on the throne where, as king, He now has all authority in heaven and in earth. He will continue interceding for those who believe in Him until the end of the age. And since His intercession is based upon His once-for-all sacrifice it is never unavailing.

(4) The privileges He obtained for believers

These are many and great. For the present we shall note only three aspects of salvation. First there is *refuge*. The Bible describes the unforgiven sinner as exposed to the wrath of God directed against all ungodliness and unrighteousness. Whoever he may be, apart from a change in his relation to God, he is without hope of escaping irrevocable condemnation. But in the verses preceding the text we read of those who fled for refuge to seize the hope offered.

That hope is securely grounded in Christ's priestly intercession, which guarantees protection forever from the condemnation and penalty due to sin. It is the sole and sufficient hope of the sinner. Consideration of a further privilege will show how he may come to possess it.

Secondly there is *reconciliation*. Christ by His sacrifice made reconciliation on behalf of sinners and we are invited to avail ourselves of it. The Gospel is called the word of reconciliation. It brings to men the thrilling news that God in love sent His Son to be the propitiation for their sins, and is prepared to welcome sinners seeking mercy as though they were righteous, on the ground of what Christ has done. But the Gospel does more than reveal encouraging facts. It appeals to us with a note of urgency to act upon these facts. "Be ye reconciled to God" (2 Cor. 5:20). "Today, if ye will hear his voice harden not your hearts" (Heb. 4:7). This involves repentance and willingness to receive a change of heart. Isaiah sheds light upon it. "Let the wicked forsake his way, and the unrighteous man his thoughts and let him return unto the Lord, and he will have mercy upon him. . . . For my thoughts are not your thoughts, neither are your ways my ways, saith the Lord" (Isa. 55:7/8). And like the father in the parable, who ran to meet his returning son when he was "yet a great way off", God is ready to meet our need (Luke 15:20). He grants repentance to those who ask it and promises an everlasting covenant assuring forgiveness, spiritual renewal and continual grace to all who return to Him and entrust themselves to Christ as Saviour.

Thirdly there is *rest*. The writer of the Epistle devotes much space to the thought of rest. As, long ago, God promised rest to Israel, the Gospel invites us today to find peace, and satisfaction in trusting, obeying and serving Christ. Yet this does not exhaust the writer's teaching on rest. Human life is transitory. The world as we know it will come to an end. But Christ's death has secured for His servants an eternal inheritance in an enduring kingdom, where sin will no more destroy their peace nor will death terminate their happy fellowship and service.

Refuge, reconciliation, rest now and rest eternal, all may

be yours, if you receive Christ as your High Priest and, by grace, give Him whole-hearted allegiance as King. For He is "the author of eternal salvation to all them that obey him" (Heb. 5:9).

W. J. CAMERON

THE WAY BACK TO GOD

"If my people, which are called by my name, shall humble themselves, and pray, and seek my face, and turn from their wicked ways; then I will hear from heaven, and will forgive their sin, and will heal their land."   2 CHR. 7:14

The chapter in which our text is found forms part of an account of a memorable day in the history of the children of Israel, namely, the day on which Solomon's temple was dedicated. It was a day which would not be forgotten readily by those who were privileged to be present, for God seemed to be very near, and in token of His presence and His approval He gave a manifestation of His glory. The enthusiasm of the people as they offered their sacrifices appeared to know no bounds; but God knew the fickleness of the human heart, and so on this day of national rejoicing when the people with unrestrained fervour proclaimed their allegiance to Him, He foresaw a time when there would be spiritual declension which would bring His judgment on the land.

This promise was made in the first instance to those whom God describes as "my people", that is, Israel as a nation. Israel had been chosen by God to be a nation which would be distinct from all other nations and, as such, was the heir of many promises. The Apostle Paul reminds us at a later date that "they are not all Israel who are of Israel", and yet I take it that the promise in our text embraced the nation as a whole. In like manner in these days in which we live God has His Church as distinct from the world, but not all those who profess to be members of the Church have been regenerated by His Holy Spirit. Yet there is a promise which embraces the whole of the visible Church; God still calls us, through His inspired Word, to return to Him, the King and Head of His own Church.

Four steps are outlined for those who would set their faces towards the road which leads back to God and the first of these is:

(1) The need for humility

"If my people shall humble themselves". Pride is one of the most common of human failings and yet it is a deadly sin. I heard a psychiatrist say recently that nowadays the seven deadly sins are minimized, and that pride, for example, is often described as "confidence in one's own ability". But call it by whatever name we will, pride is still that ugly thing which causes puny man to shake his fist in the face of Almighty God, and say, "I am the master of my fate; I am the captain of my soul". When a soul is humbled in the presence of God, however, this blustering attitude retreats into the background and the soul will be prepared to make acknowledgment of certain things. To begin with, there will be an acknowledgment of sin. Sin will be seen in its true colours as a "want of conformity unto, and transgression of, the law of God". It will no longer be explained away in such terms as "an error of judgment", or "a mistake", but will be recognized as an act of rebellion. Moreover, the wrong which is done through sin will be regarded as a wrong not merely against one's fellow, but against God. In the spirit of true humility the penitent soul will say, as the Psalmist did, "Against thee, thee only, have I sinned, and done this evil in thy sight . . ." (Ps. 51:4).

Coupled with this acknowledgment of sin there will be an acknowledgment of failure. It is characteristic of the man whose religion is a mere formality that he is generally well satisfied with his own attainments. The standard which he adopts is man-made, and by this standard he compares very favourably with his fellows. "I'm as good as other men and a good deal better than most of them", he is heard to say, as he seeks to boost his morale. On the contrary the man who stands humbled in the presence of God is stripped of his self-assurance and readily admits that he has been "weighed in the balances and found wanting". "Man's chief end," he remembers, "is to glorify God", and as he contemplates his own weak efforts he realizes how little he has achieved towards the fulfilment of this end. A saintly man said to me recently, "I shall not be afraid to meet my Maker for I am resting on the finished work of Christ, but when I think of how little I have done for Him I shall be ashamed to look Him in the face". And these are the sentiments of all who have learned the secret of true humility.

Arising out of this sense of sin and failure there will also be an acknowledgment of need. When the eyes of men are opened by the grace of God they are conscious not only of a sense of sin but also of their need of divine help, and they are ready to say with Augustus Toplady:

> Not the labours of my hands
> Can fulfil Thy law's demands;
> Could my zeal no respite know,
> Could my tears for ever flow,
> All for sin could not atone:
> Thou must save, and Thou alone.

(2) The need for prayer

Humbled in the presence of God by a sense of his own unworthiness, the subject of grace will moreover recognize his need of divine help as he faces the trials and temptations of life. If his own efforts are futile to effect his justification, they are equally futile to promote sanctification; and so, with an enlightened mind, he implores the aid of the Divine Helper. Thus by humility the mind is conditioned for the exercise of prayer, which is the next essential on the road to spiritual recovery.

When Saul of Tarsus was brought to the house of Ananias following his conflict with the risen Christ on the road to Damascus it was recorded of him, "Behold, he prayeth". This was no new occupation for Saul, for as a Pharisee he was well accustomed to the regular routine of prayer. But now his prayers were no longer a mere formality but a tremendous reality. They were the utterances of a man who had been humbled into saying, "Lord, what wilt thou have me to do?". Surely there is a worthwhile lesson for us here. The Church of God needs to be shaken out of her formality and to recapture the spirit of true prayer. That noted preacher of last century, Charles Haddon Spurgeon, used to describe the weekly prayer meeting as "the heating apparatus of the Church". Yet in how many churches today the heating apparatus is never turned on! It is little wonder then that we find such a low spiritual temperature in our midst. The embers of the fire of our spiritual life are burning so low that they fail to bring comfort and cheer to people who seek these, and perplexed and disillusioned men and women are turning their back upon the Church because it has nothing to offer to them. Wherein then lies the remedy for the apathy and apostasy of this present age? "If my people," says God, ". . . shall . . . pray . . . then will I . . . heal their land".

(3) The need for earnestness

A further essential requirement on the part of those who seek the way back to God is earnestness. They must "seek my face", says God. It is surprising how many people who are intensely earnest and persevering in their attitude to problems concerning their material welfare are casual almost to an equal degree in regard to spiritual matters. During the last world war when many commodities were in short supply in Britain, the only way to procure certain articles was to take one's place in the line, and it became a common sight to see long queues in our streets. Consequently many people developed a "queue complex", and some were even known to take their place without knowing what they were waiting for. The obvious reason was that they were afraid they would miss something. What a tremendous difference it would make to the life of the Church if its members showed the same concern in regard to spiritual things! There would always be crowded congregations because men and women would be afraid to remain away from services lest they miss a blessing. Thomas was not present on that first occasion when the risen Christ revealed Himself to His disciples in the Upper Room, and as a result we can believe that for a time, at least, his witness was impaired because his mind was clouded by doubts and fears. And who can deny that many today find themselves in "Doubting Castle", and are not contributing as they should to the life

22

and witness of the Church because they are not frequently enough in the company of Jesus.

Another practice to which those who lived in wartime Britain grew accustomed was that of granting priority. Certain projects were regarded as more important than others, and there was little prospect of any work being undertaken unless it appeared on a priority list. What we are all too inclined to forget, however, is that the Lord has provided a priority list, and right at the head of that list is the very thing which our text counsels us to do. "Seek ye first", says Christ, "the kingdom of God, and his righteousness; and all these things shall be added unto you" (Matt. 6:33). Yet many professing Christians are so deeply concerned with things which should be of secondary importance that they have little or no time left in which to "seek the Lord"; and as a consequence their spiritual growth becomes stunted. Is it not time then for all of us to check up on our priorities and to ensure that the Lord is given his rightful place in our hearts and lives? And remembering that this is an urgent matter, let us do it now. In days of old the prophet Hosea sent forth a clarion call to backsliding Israel, and surely his words are apposite to the times in which we live: "Sow to yourselves in righteousness," he says, "reap in mercy; break up your fallow ground; for it is time to seek the Lord, till he come and rain righteousness upon you" (Hos. 10:12).

(4) The need for renouncing evil

The remaining condition which was required of Israel as a harbinger of blessing was a renunciation of evil: they were to "turn from their wicked ways". It is surprising that a people who had been chosen by God should be so ready to turn their backs upon him. Yet the Israelites were all too prone to follow the heathen nations round about them and to engage in, among other things, the practice of idolatry. From their history we learn that time and time again they forsook the living God and worshipped the gods of the heathen, and we are confronted with such sorry spectacles as that which greeted Moses when he came down from the mount and found the people, for whom God had effected a

23

great deliverance, bowing down and worshipping a golden calf.

Unfortunately the practice of idolatry has not ceased with the passing of the years, and while it is true that we may no longer worship golden calves, as Israel did, yet there are many idols to which men do homage and, as a result, Christ is dethroned. How many there are, who, like the rich young ruler, are making wealth their God. In this material age in which everything is measured in terms of pounds or dollars, we may sometimes even be found guilty of assessing spiritual progress by the offerings of the people. It is true, of course, that where there is real spiritual life there will be sacrificial giving, but it is all too possible for a church to glory in her financial achievements rather than in her Lord. Like the church in Laodicea she may be "rich and increased with goods" and think that she has "need of nothing", not knowing she is "wretched and miserable, and poor, and blind, and naked".

Another idol of which we must ever beware is popularity or the approval of men. We tend to become so afraid lest we may be thought odd or different from our fellows, and, as a consequence, the voice of the Church is not raised as often as it should be against moral evil. When situations arise as they so often do when professing Christians are called upon to take a stand for righteousness and truth, or to denounce that which is wrong, the voice of Christian witness is often silenced because the approval of men counts more than the approval of God. And so by our very silence we become partakers of their wicked ways. One of the dangers of this ecumenical age is that ecumenicity itself may become an idol, and that the Church, in order to win the approval of men and to maintain the spirit of unity among those whose views may be widely divergent, is tempted to compromise those great truths of which she has been made custodian. Is it any wonder then that the man of the world becomes perplexed and bewildered as he seeks to ascertain what the Church believes and what benefits she has to offer him which he does not already possess? And the sad outcome is that all too often with a shrug of his shoulder he dismisses the Christian faith as something which is not relevant to the

24

world of today. Undoubtedly there is need for Christian unity, but it must be a unity which has as its foundation an uncompromising belief in the Incarnation and finished work of the Divine Saviour who said, "I, if I be lifted up . . ., will draw all men unto me".

(5) The blessings assured

Two blessings are promised to those who fulfil God's requirements. The first of these is a personal blessing and consists of pardon—"I will forgive their sin". How gracious God is, both to the sinner and to the backsliding Christian. For the sinner who forsakes his ways and turns unto the Lord there is abundant pardon, and for the backslider who confesses his sins there is forgiveness and cleansing.

But notice that there is also a promise of national blessing—"I will heal their land". God had warned Israel that one of the consequences of sin would be drought. "It may be necessary," He said, "to shut up heaven that there be no rain". Israel's very existence depended on "the former and latter rains", for without them there would be famine in the land. During the reign of Ahab the land experienced a sore famine, and only after the prayers of Elijah was the famine brought to an end, and the land healed.

Is there not much to remind us that the same healing power is needed in our land today? We live in times of spiritual drought and barrenness and urgently need those refreshing showers which alone can revive the parched ground. The world is in a state of tension and men's hearts are failing them for fear. But let us not forget that God has promised blessing when men turn to Him in penitence and faith.

Do you wish then to make a contribution to the national effort which can have far-reaching consequences? Do you wish to see that "righteousness which exalteth a nation" established in the land? Do you wish to see the "windows of heaven" opened and the blessing poured out? Here then are the conditions! "If my people, which are called by my name, shall humble themselves, and pray, and seek my face, and turn from their wicked ways; then will I hear from heaven, and will forgive their sin, and will heal their land." If we by His grace are willing and able to fulfil the conditions, God will surely honour His promise.

W. R. Mackay

BUILT ON THE ROCK

"Upon this rock I will build my Church; and the gates of hell shall not prevail against it."　　　　　MATT. 16:18

When Jesus uttered these words to Peter at Caesarea Philippi He was entering the final phase of His earthly ministry; a phase that was to be very different from the earlier ones; that was to see His popularity diminish, the crowds depart and the shadows of the Cross deepen around Him. It was then He began the process of preparing His disciples for the swift series of events which was to culminate in the Cross: Preparing them for the crisis which would face them as their faith came under the crucible-test of His own death and departure from them. And He took the first step in that process when He asked them the question, 'Whom do men say that I, the Son of Man, am?" (Matt. 16:13).

Note His method. He first of all draws from them the erroneous and conflicting opinions of unbelief and then, against that background, has them confess their own conception of who He is. And the contrast drawn between the two outlooks is so immediate, so vivid in outline and sharp in focus, that the full implication of their own testimony is established and driven home to their hearts with one master-stroke. The disciples told Him what men were saying. And what marks these popular views is their utter lack of unanimity. "Some say that thou art John the Baptist; some, Elias; and others, Jeremias, or one of the prophets" (v. 14). These were the conflicting opinions of speculative thought and their discord stands in complete contrast to the harmony of those taught of God. There, one voice can speak for all, and one voice does. Peter does not say, "Well, this is John's view, and this is James's view and this Andrew's, and my own differs from them all". No!

27

"Thou art the Christ, the Son of the living God", said Peter, and he voiced the thought of every heart.

When the Lord comments on this testimony—and, incidentally, this was the opportune moment for Him to banish forever any wrong conception from their minds and the fact that He did not do so testifies to His full Messianic self-consciousness—when He comments on the testimony, He reveals its true source. Peter's confession was due, not to his own powers of insight or penetrating discernment but to the revelation of God. Jesus wishes these men—and believing men in every age—to know that their faith stands, and shall stand, not "in the wisdom of men", but in "the power of God" (1 Cor. 2:5).

Then, Christ proceeds to unfold the significance of their testimony to the disciples. And first, He demonstrates that significance in relation to Peter himself. Simon gets a new name, outward symbol of the new nature that the confession implies. But He does not stop at Peter in unfolding the significance of this confession. He illustrates its meaning and relevance in relation to all believers, and that illustration, and the great truth which it highlights, we have in the words of our text.

(1) The enduring stability of the Church of Christ

The major factor in the stability of any building is the foundation and this is where Christ first directs attention. "Upon this 'ROCK' will I build my church."

So much has been written on the controversy that has raged around this phrase that there is no need, here, to set out proof that the rock is not Peter but the confession that Peter made, or more precisely, the Christ that Peter confessed. I just remark in the passing that if the reference were to Peter then the manner of expression used here would be extremely indirect and unnatural. The rock is Christ, the One to Whom Peter has just borne such striking testimony.

Look at that testimony again, for it stands related to what Jesus says of the stability of His church. "Thou art the Christ, the Son of the living God", said Peter. These words centre on a relationship: the Sonship of Jesus to the living God. And it is within that circle of relationship that Christ

28

claims to be the "rock" on which His church is founded. It is the relation He sustains to God that Peter has confessed and, on the basis of that confession, Jesus elucidates and establishes the relation He sustains to His church. He is, in fact, accepting and confirming a confession of His Own Deity and Eternal Sonship. The words of Peter, "Living God" should be noted, for it is the expression that the Jew used to mark off Jehovah, in contrast to the idols of heathen nations, as the sovereign, self-existent, Creator: the One Whose being is completely underived: the One of Whom Jesus Himself says, "The Father hath life in Himself" (John 5:26). That is the importance of the relationship announced in Peter's confession and confirmed by Christ's reply.

Now, two things are implied in the thought of this Sonship, and they help us substantiate from His own teaching the fact that Christ did make the claim to Deity. There is identity of nature and identity of life in the thought. And, that is what Jesus did teach of His own relationship to God. "For as the Father hath life in Himself, so hath He given the Son to have life in Himself" (John 5:26). We cannot doubt that the Jews recognized this as a claim to Divine nature and Divine life, for, when He asserted it they accused Him of blasphemy, "Because He made Himself equal with God" (John 5:18). Standing in the very same tradition, Peter must have been just as sensitive to what the claim involved as were the accusers and that fact underlines the certitude of his conviction and the grandeur of his confession.

Let us bear in mind another factor which reveals the strength of Peter's confession and testimony. The Divinity of Jesus is part of our theological thought-structure, but it was not so with Peter. He first knew Jesus as a man, and as a man among men. He knew the place of His birth, he knew Mary His mother and he knew His brothers. Peter had seen Him tired and weary; had seen Him mourn and weep, and hunger and thirst, just like other men. Peter knew Him in the familiarity of everyday contact—and how often sheer closeness like this can blunt perception and blur vision!—but even through this familiarity with Jesus

29

as a man, Peter's faith reached to take hold of this other truth, "Here is the Son of God". "Whom do men say that I, the Son of MAN am?" and, as heaven's light flashed into his soul Peter saw this grand truth. The Son of Man IS the Son of God.

But Peter's testimony was not only to the Person of this Son, but to His work also. "THOU art the CHRIST". He saw that Jesus of Nazareth was not only the Son, but the Servant of Jehovah. The Ordained and Anointed and Sent One. The One promised in Old Testament prophecy and pre-figured in its sacrifice and ceremony. His confession thrills through with his recognition of the "Hope of Israel". He saw Jesus now, not alone for who He really was, but also for what He had come to do.

This is where the Church is founded. This is the platform of her enduring stability. She is rooted, not in the visions and labours of men of faith but in the Person and Work of the Eternal Son Himself. Her life flows from the One Who has life in Himself and Who, having life in Himself, had the authority to lay it down and the ability to take it again, actively providing both the purchase price and the saving power of her eternal redemption. "On this rock I will build my church." And, let everyone who is a part of the Church through faith in Jesus be unafraid, for it is the rock of Enduring Stability.

(2) The envisaged structure of the Church of Christ

"I will build my church." The thought is illustrative of His church as a building and it is a thought that leads to three remarks about the Church.

There is, first of all, the thought of personal possession. Behind every building is a person. A person who plans and prepares and builds. That is precisely the emphasis here. "My" church. "I" will build. There is a tremendous sense of assurance and possession about that: of purpose and determination. My "Church", even although, as He spoke that church was only a handful of country followers. But, as Jesus looked at these few, what did He see? His church! And He saw His church because His eye looked on from that hour at Caesarea Philippi, on through the coming centuries, and contemplated the building in all the glory of its completion. He saw, not merely the plan, not just the foundation, but He saw the building in its full realisation. He saw the "Lively stones" come from every nation, tribe and tongue and they were as "the sand on the seashore for multitude". And, He saw the walls reared up straight, and stately and strong; He saw every stone hewn and shaped and fitted in place and then, surely, He saw the great head-stone itself, "brought forth with shouting" and He heard the songs of acclamation . . . "salvation to our God which sitteth upon the throne, and unto the Lamb . . . blessing and glory" (Rev. 7:10, 12).

That was His vision when He said that great thing, "I will build my church". And it was His vision because it was His purpose and His Father's purpose. The purpose that He was, even then, in the process of fulfilling; fulfilling by way of obedience; by way of suffering; by way of death. And, through all the way of His perfect obedience, through the agony of the garden and the suffering of the Cross, that purpose can be read and re-read unchanged, "I will build my church". The vision girdled the purpose and so our Redeemer, "For the joy that was set before Him, endured the Cross, despising the shame" (Heb. 12:2). And, as we look to Him in faith we can also be strong, for He will build His church, He is building His church, and one day the structure will stand complete.

That leads to a second remark about the Church, and it is simply this. The Church of Christ is a living structure, and points to the thought of a living fellowship. The Greek original, "Ecclesia" means a group of people who are "Called", or "Called out", and so, when we think of the Church in this New Testament sense of the word we have to dismiss any thought of buildings or organisations from our minds and think of it as a group of living persons who have been called by the Holy Spirit into fellowship with Christ and with one another.

It is good, in these days of ecumenical ferment, that we remember this fact. For, it teaches us where the true unity of the Church really centres. The question that lies at the heart of the matter is not what organization a man may belong to but whether, by the grace of God, he has been called into the living fellowship of the Church that Christ is building. That, and not his connection among men, is what makes a Christian!

This takes us to the third remark about the Church. It is Christ who builds. And that, I think, is a thought of great tenderness. When we remember how Jesus dealt with people, then we can be trusting and unafraid. The very thought of another having absolute sovereignty over us can be overwhelming, but when we remember who it is that wields this power then there is no place for fear. "I will build", and He reserves the work for Himself; He delegates it to no one else. Every time He touches our lives to shape us for the building—and the hewing can be a sore process sometimes—His touch carries with it His own tender word, "Be not afraid, it is I". His is the touch of love, of perfect love, and, "Perfect love casteth out fear, for there is no fear in love" (1 John 4:18). The thought carries not only tenderness, but assurance. Of this builder and His great task the prophet said, "He shall not fail nor be discouraged" (Isa. 42:4), and the psalmist sang, "He shall have dominion also from sea to sea, and from the river unto the ends of the earth" (Ps. 72:8).

(3) The eternal security of the Church of Christ

Mark how strongly Christ puts this security. "The gates of hell shall not prevail against it."

That expression, "The gates of hell' is by some regarded as being the mere equivalent of the word "hell". Taken so, the words just mean that the Church shall never perish, it has certainty of life. But, while that is a very wonderful truth taught elsewhere in Scripture, I do not think it is the main truth taught us here. There is the plain idea of conflict in the word "prevail". It enshrines the idea of a consistent purpose to storm and destroy; to attack the Church with a strong, persistent onslaught. Add to this the fact that, in Biblical times, the "gates of the city" were the places where important business was done; where the elders met to deliberate and pass judgment and hold councils of war until the expression came to have a specific, technical usage, and to mean collective experience, wisdom and skill, and we can begin to understand how strong the thing Jesus said really was. Plainly, He was asserting that although the total resources of hell, the cunning and evil and malice of the marshalled forces of Satan, were to be pitted against His Church, they would not prevail nor conquer.

The Church does not just contend against flesh and blood—these are often against her—but her most formidable foe is Satan himself. Paul, in his letter to the church at Ephesus, puts it very strongly, "We wrestle not against flesh and blood, but against principalities, against powers ... against spiritual wickedness in high places" (Eph. 6:12). Well, this word of Christ is a promise for the Church and so, for every individual member of it. Every believer can draw strength from this. Though hell pit all its resources against us—and down through the centuries hell has done that—the building of Christ stands sure, having this seal, "The Lord knoweth them that are His" (2 Tim. 2:19). No weapon forged against this building can prosper. Nothing from the armoury of Satan can destroy one of Christ's people, for their "life is hid with Christ in God" (Col. 3:3). What utter security belongs to those who are called into Christ and so into His Church, for, "The gates of hell shall not prevail against it".

Let me sum up, in conclusion, the teaching of our text. Three things are vital to the lasting strength of any building. The first is the foundation. No building is any stronger than its found. Let all who have been brought into Christ's Church by the regenerating power of the Holy Spirit remember, always, the rock that is the fortress and foundation of her stability: nothing less than Christ Himself, in all the glory of His person and His Work. With Jeremiah we can look up and say, "A glorious high throne from the beginning, is the place of our sanctuary" (Jer. 17:12).

The second factor in the strength of a building is this. The workman who erects the structure. On his character, on his honesty, on his integrity on his skill and his craftsmanship hangs the whole future of the building. And, this workman is none other than the Master-builder Himself. This is the One in whom, and by whom, "All the building, fitly framed together, groweth unto an holy temple in the Lord" (Eph. 2:21).

The third thing in the strength and lasting security of a building is its power of resistance to the destructive elements of nature. By what power is the Church of Jesus Christ preserved from destruction? Peter himself tells us. The believer is, he says, "Kept by the power of God, through faith, unto salvation" (1 Pet. 1:5).

The ultimate question with which we each, as individuals, have to deal is just this: are we, ourselves, within the safety of Christ's true Church? Have we trusted the salvation of our souls to Him? This is the very Saviour of whom Peter was later to preach—and, let me urge the point of his sermon in his own words—"There is none other name under heaven given among men whereby we must be saved" (Acts 4:12). All who know Him as Saviour, all who have trusted Him, find rest and peace in Him. He is the One who carries toward fruition the redemptive accomplishment that stood clear to His gaze as He made this great assertion, "I will build my Church and the gates of hell shall not prevail against it". There is our confidence: there is the measure of our Christian hope: there we may trust, and not be afraid.

J. D. MACMILLAN

FACING THE DARK DAYS

2 TIM. 4:9–22

Paul's placement of Timothy as pastor–superintendent of the Christian community at Ephesus with its complex of always difficult and sometimes very vexatious problems was an interesting one. Timothy had been of course specially set apart and endowed for the work of an evangelist by the laying on of the hands both of Paul and of the presbytery. He had already given excellent service to the apostle as his missionary companion over a considerable period, and had been sent as his trusted delegate on a variety of short-term missions to encourage and to steady churches which were facing serious internal problems or else bearing the heat of persecution. There was in Timothy, too, something which appeared to Paul to fit him pre-eminently for the sort of work which Ephesus would demand. Speaking to the Philippians he said of Timothy, "I have no man likeminded who will naturally care for your state. For all seek their own, not the things which are Jesus Christ's. But ye know him that as a son with the father he hath served with me in the Gospel" (Phil. 2:20–22). Leaving aside the minute details of interpretation, this tribute identified Timothy as someone possessed to a quite remarkable degree of unselfish and genuine Christian concern for the welfare of his fellow-believers and equally for the furtherance of the missionary enterprises of the Church; and as going far beyond the general run of Christians in devotion to the Lord Jesus Christ. Indeed, if we take the apostle's language literally, the description of Timothy was that he figured as a "co-slave" of Christ along with Paul himself.

On the other hand, Timothy was now faced with an unusually stiff and long-term exercise in missionary organization. Of him Paul expected the establishment of the Ephesian church on a regular basis, the appointment and the training of officials as a main step in that direction, and the combating of a particularly subtle and also stubborn collection of false teachers. All this from a man who was still young, timid by disposition, frequently unwell and subject, we can gather, to depression, and deprived at a critical juncture of the benefit of the apostle's close supervision and advice.

We shall consider four of the main-line reasons offered by Paul as inducements to Timothy to apply himself both vigorously and unfalteringly to his assignment in Ephesus.

(1) The second coming of Christ the righteous judge

"I charge thee before God and the Lord Jesus Christ, who shall judge the quick and the dead at his appearing and his kingdom, Preach the word, etc."

The general idea is that Timothy, if he is faithful to the charge about to be developed by Paul, will share in the glory of Christ's coming and reign.

The servants of Christ are bound to concern themselves at all points in their Christian life and service with the solemn fact that we must one day every one of us give an account to Christ the righteous judge. And the consideration that even now the quality of our work is open to the scrutiny of heaven is stressed in the words, "I charge thee in the presence of God and the Lord Jesus Christ".

At the same time the Lord Jesus Christ is to be regarded as the unfailing Saviour of His people, as He is also their loved and respected Master, to give pleasure to whom must rank as a high incentive to offer the best in service. It belongs to Him to bring the good work He has begun in His people and which also He prosecutes through them to perfect fruition. He is the righteous judge (v. 8) who will make certain that the righteous man shall not fail of a proper and glorious reward; even if circumstances on earth may seem at times likely to frustrate it.

For Timothy, especially in the dark days which he was destined to face, there would come inevitably the temptation to view his work as a monotonous and meaningless round of routine procedures, or on the other hand as an unavailing series of distressing encounters with the forces of evil. It was imperative therefore that he should keep before him the truth that Christ is in undisputed charge of the Gospel's onward movement.

(2) The proper Christian reaction to dark and difficult times

Dark and difficult days were on the way for the apostolic church, and in Ephesus, notably, the threatening clouds were already hanging low over the Christian scene. "The time will come"—Paul is completely frank with Timothy—"when they will not endure sound doctrine; but after their own lusts they heap to themselves teachers, having itching ears: And they shall turn away from the truth and shall be turned unto fables". Yet the last thing that we might expect Paul to do would be to paint the picture in sombre tones merely in answer to some foreboding or other of his own heart, or because he believed a tragic cathartic experience of soul would in the end be good for Timothy. Paul had the mind of Christ and Christianity does not operate on such lines. His very next word—one of those celebrated Pauline "buts"—should alert us to something far removed from a gloomy contemplation of the turn of events for its own sake. "But watch thou in all things, endure afflictions, do the work of an evangelist, make full proof of thy ministry." The verb "watch" carries the force of the "be sober", and calls upon Timothy to maintain unruffled and alert commitment to all of his Christian undertakings, in distinction from running panic-stricken away from them. The command to endure afflictions repeats the exhortation of chapter 2:3 where Paul urges Timothy to "endure hardness as a good soldier of Jesus Christ". Because there is a war on—Christ and His Church versus Satan—Christ's followers must accept austerity and put up with hardship as rigours which are quite inseparable from the campaign, and as being experiences without which they cannot reasonably expect to share in Christ's victories. We may summarise the main points of the apostle's teaching as follows:

37

1. Christian ministers and Christian witnesses in general have, according to Paul, all the greater reason for maintaining a steady witness to the Gospel (fulfilling their ministry), all the greater reason for maintaining Christian teaching and promoting Christian evangelism vigorously and unfalteringly, in days when the professing Christian church over a wide field is unsteady and uncertain.

2. Whenever there is a general drifting away from solid Christian instruction, that is the very time to take special steps to defend and promote the doctrine of Christ. Says Paul, "preach the word", the original, undiminished Gospel of Christ. "Be instant in season, out of season": i.e. be unfailingly at your post as pastor, teacher and evangelist, whether or not the times are propitious, and whether in your immediate environment you are met with encouraging reactions or equally the reverse. And of course even a saint, proverbially, can be provoked to say and do unsaintly things. So Paul enjoins Timothy to "reprove, rebuke and exhort", by all means—in the situation emerging it would be completely necessary—but let him do it "with all long-suffering and doctrine". Christian courtesy and affectionate patience are always, under God, powerful inducements to people to give to the Gospel a reasonable hearing.

3. And do not forget to "do the work of an evangelist", is Paul's next advice. Just because the days are becoming dark, and people themselves are becoming dark in relation to Gospel truth, the duty of maintaining an evangelistic initiative, and not simply the duty of holding the Christian fort as it stands, will be of prime importance. The temptation is strong at such times for the orthodox Christian community to turn in on itself. The temptation is strong to, so to say, keep the pot of churchly activity just simmering until revival takes place. No, Paul would say, such an attitude is quite wrong. It is here and now, if ever and anywhere, when the difficult days are actually upon us, yes and growing, that Christians must address themselves to the inalienable duty of evangelizing the world.

4. Timothy, moreover, would be compelled to witness people forsaking his own faithful ministry in favour of teachers who would cater for people's "itching ears" and

who would accommodate what doctrine was offered to people's "lusts", succumbing, that is to say, right, left and centre to popular demand and suppressing in the process the Biblical insistence both on personal holiness and on the exclusive Gospel way of salvation. Timothy, however, must not be induced by that painful experience to relax either his standards or his efforts. A cheap convert here or there might easily enough be obtained. But at what a cost to his loyalty to Christ and to the true salvation of his hearers! The temptation to pique and self-pity would on such occasions too be human enough. Thus Paul recommends Timothy to "watch", to be sober, to be quite unrelenting with himself in the direction of holding to his Gospel perspectives. For the sake of genuine Gospel results he must endure such afflictions and make full proof of his ministry.

5. It is instructive, incidentally, to see how much weight Paul lays on the place of Christian doctrine, and the study of it, as a prime factor in the strengthening of Christians for their duty. "Consider what I say", he exhorts when in chapter 2 he calls upon his young colleague to behave in his Christian witness after the style of a good soldier, a dedicated athlete and an industrious farmer. "Consider what I say; and the Lord give thee understanding in all things."

This means that spiritual strength will come to the Christian through careful attention to doctrinal considerations. We have no right to expect a spiritual uplift, the surge of Christian optimistic feeling, or a better resolution to face difficult undertakings, however much we pray and however much we seek the Spirit's help, without careful and continual meditation on the teaching of Holy Scripture. The continuance of Christian courage is guaranteed only in the closest possible conjunction with the continuance of Christian Bible study.

(3) The logic of Paul's death for Timothy his colleague and successor

Paul produces further support for the charge which he gives to Timothy to be faithful to his ministry from the fact that he himself is now ready to die as Christ's martyr. "Watch thou in all things, endure afflictions, do the work of an evangelist, make full proof of thy ministry: For I am now ready to be offered, and the time of my departure is at hand." The duty of faithfulness on Timothy's part takes on urgency from the impending removal of his senior colleague from the missionary scene.

The apostle saw no virtue in concealing the fact from Timothy that the old and cherished partnership between them was on the point of being broken up irretrievably. Such concealment would at best have secured only a cheap and short-lived and paper-thin protection from reality for young Timothy. For himself, distasteful the mere article of death, and such a death, might be—he had above all else a sense of grateful satisfaction at having, in Christ's strength, fought a good fight, and finished his course and kept the faith. And he had nothing but confident expectation of receiving from Christ's own hands the victor's crown. One or two points are deserving of special notice.

1. Here, Paul's steady purpose throughout the epistle, that of urging Timothy on so as to give his ministry in Ephesus his undivided and active attention, is not for one minute being forgotten by him. The apostle has not suddenly turned autobiographical in any sort of isolation from what he has been saying. He is not even preparing Timothy simply for his death so that the young man will not be too personally upset when it actually happens. No, rather like a wounded field commander whose own time on the battle-ground is about up, he is anxious to devote the short time that is left him to deploying the forces still on the field to maximum advantage. The leadership is being transferred from the shoulders of the aged apostle to that of his youthful subordinate. The last thing Paul wants Timothy to do is to give way to overmuch sorrow as a result of his chief's departure from the scene. And he has in mind the furtherance of the Gospel's cause even more than concern for Timothy's personal comfort.

2. If the removal by death of the admired and loved leaders of one generation, people on whom we have so much depended in earlier days, has this effect upon us, that it inspires us to take up those duties upon which the once strong but now nerveless fingers have finally lost their

grasp, and urges us to view more seriously than ever before
our existing Christian work, then it is well. Paul would
approve.

3. In Paul's martyr testimony there is implicit the assurance that Timothy too, with the same divine help, will
succeed in fighting the good fight, in finishing his own
course, and in keeping the faith, let the forces of evil at
Ephesus, or anywhere else, do their worst. Timothy will
require not to be taken off his guard, and not to think that
some strange thing is happening to him, by the discovery
that there is a fierce fight to be fought, and a strenuous race
to be run, and that the faith has to be kept inviolate when
profane hands reach out to wrench his testimony away from
him. Paul's God will prove to be Timothy's God throughout.

(4) The implications of Paul's attitude to the ex-
perience of loneliness

Paul at Rome was as open to the temptations projected
by loneliness and the painful experience of desertion as
any man. It is a cry from the heart of a Christian man in
great need of fellowship when he says to Timothy, "Do thy
diligence to come shortly to me. . . . Do thy diligence to
come before winter." Certainly he had good friends over-
seas, some of whom he specially mentions: Prisca and Aquila
and the household of Onesiphorus. They were at Ephesus
with Timothy, as possibly by now was Tychicus. Several of
the others he mentions were away on far-flung missionary
errands: Crescens, Titus and Erastus. Demas had disloyally
forsaken him. Trophimus he had left at Miletum, sick. Luke
was with him indeed, but he could scarcely keep Paul
company all the time, nor assist him with every problem.
Eubulus, Pudens, Linus and Claudia and "all the brethren",
who no doubt had visited him at one time or another, and
were resident in Rome, must have been limited in their con-
tacts with him—perhaps (in the light of v. 16) too often from
fear. They were probably not able in any case to provide the
sort of fellowship which a man of Timothy's calibre,
experience and closeness to Paul could provide at this
juncture.

This allows an interesting commentary on fairly normal

Christian experience. How often in a trying situation does the Christian who may be at the height of his devotion to the Gospel of Christ nevertheless find himself deprived of helpful fellowship. Some of his best Christian friends—the ones who could be of most value at the time—are in some distant place: or are perhaps sick. The result is the same. And those Christians who are nearer at hand and mobile are either not presently available or are not for some reason capable of giving the quality and the degree of sympathetic encouragement necessary. And how specially painful when some previous fellow-campaigner (like Demas) has walked out on one, having succumbed perhaps to the attraction of worldly considerations. Paul was not complaining. Rather was he illustrating his need, and forewarning Timothy at the same time that this might very well be his line of experience sooner or later. Timothy must thus be prepared to take his share of the hardship which one way or another was inseparable from being a servant of Christ (1:8).

Faced with this situation Paul asked Timothy for three items of help, and each separate request made is not without instruction for all Christians.

1. *Company*. Timothy was to come himself bringing Mark as well, and he was to do so before the winter storms would make sailing out of the question. One Commentator underlines at this point the interesting fact that Paul who "loved the appearing of Christ" (v. 8) longed at the same time for the coming of Timothy. It is being more spiritual than the apostle Paul!—for people to claim that they can dispense with human fellowship since they have Christ. We neglect Christian fellowship at our peril. Christ ministers to His people through their Christian friends. And we require to adjust our doctrine of the Holy Spirit, the Comforter, by the apostolic doctrine implicit in this chapter that that same Holy Spirit generally comforts the Christian through the fellowship of other Christians.

There is this point too. Paul had earlier in life enjoyed marvellous fellowship with the apostles and other members of the apostolic missionary establishment. But those days were past. Darker, more deprived, more meagre days, so far as Gospel fellowship was concerned, had arrived. Paul knew well enough also that he could not put the clock back. He could not return simply through wistful reflection to the earlier state of affairs. But what we find him actually doing was developing what fellowship he could by inviting Timothy and Mark to come and join him for that purpose. And Christians in our own time, some of them able to recall days of outstanding fellowship, instead of wistfully harking back for ever to those days would be better employed in taking steps to develop fellowship on a more modest scale here and now, and wherever possible.

2. *Warm clothing*. Paul owned an overcoat which—whether with typical ministerial forgetfulness or not!—he had left with his friend Carpus at Troas. With the winter temperatures even of Rome in mind he foresaw that it would be a handy article to have by him. He did not expect the Lord to work miracles unnecessarily. Timothy could stop off at Troas and collect the coat for him. As well as catering in an obvious way for his own need, Paul may very well have been serving advice to Timothy, who had certain impractical weaknesses in his make-up, never to undervalue the factor of common-sense in the pursuit of his ministry.

It is not unreasonable to suppose in the present context that apart from making a very effective gesture towards forestalling a loss of body temperature, which if it happened would also complicate his temptation to feel deprived and forlorn, the apostle Paul, knowing his man and well aware that there would be others like him to follow, was consciously placing an instructive estimate before Timothy on the importance of being practical in the Christian life. Getting things done that need to be done, however down-to-earth their nature, is not at all unrelated to the further-ance of the most spiritual objects of the Gospel as a whole. And the calculus of level-headedness, given its proper place by the Christian alongside the doctrinal and spiritual interests of his life, cannot but enhance his preparedness for the Lord's next call upon him.

3. *Books and parchments*. This could conceivably refer to the Old Testament Scriptures and to some of Paul's corre-spondence. We cannot be sure. Calvin comments that "this passage commends continual reading to all godly men as a

thing from which they can profit". It may well be costly in terms of loss of morale and of a sense of Christian purpose for any Christian to be twiddling his thumbs or doing something else equally ineffective, when he might be getting down to some worthwhile reading.

Finally, the apostle's testimony to the Lord's standing by him when, for whatever reason, he had been deserted by his Christian friends at his first appearance before Nero, is intended without doubt for Timothy's special attention as the pastor-evangelist in Ephesus. Such forsaking could happen—might very well happen—to him too. In that event the Lord would stand by him, as He had stood by Paul.

The Lord had however done more for Paul on that occasion than supply him with courage and protection and suitable words of defence. He had strengthened him so that "all the Gentiles might hear". We may suppose that it was not simply Caesar and the officials of court and the military escort who were present at the trial. There would very likely have gathered a large assembly of curious onlookers. And what the Lord did precisely was supply Paul in his most grievous misfortune with the largest congregation of Gentiles he had been privileged to address in many a long day, and equip him to present to them a very full account of the Gospel of Christ. And the same Lord, let Timothy take note, was able and ready in his case too to turn his sorest strait into an effective Gospel opportunity.

Not only this but Paul was satisfied that the Lord would "deliver him from every evil work, and preserve him unto his heavenly kingdom." Paul did not allow himself to think that the successful negotiation of one severe onslaught from evil sources was the end of that story. There would be more and very likely worse to come for himself, yes and for Timothy too. But what did it matter? The Lord had delivered his servant "in six troubles: yea and in seven there should no evil touch him." It was for Timothy to grasp (it is for all Christians to grasp), that everlasting salvation is the birthright of every believer. For every successive evil work—its proportions do not matter— there is more than ample deliverance held in readiness by the Lord to meet the evil. Timothy had every conceivable reason for making full proof of his ministry in hope and confidence.

H. CAMERON

HOLDING THE FAITH

"Hold fast the form of sound words, which thou hast heard of me, in faith and love which is in Christ Jesus. That good thing which was committed unto thee keep by the Holy Ghost which dwelleth in us."
2 TIM. 1:13, 14

There is no hint of a generation gap in the relationship between old Paul and young Timothy. Out of deep affection and in terms of their common loyalty to the Saviour Paul speaks freely and frankly to his younger colleague; his topics including the deep mysteries of the faith, the supervision of the churches and the qualities of church leaders, and practical everyday things like money, sex and idle chatter.

Inevitably, Paul's fondness for Timothy expresses itself in terms of gratitude for the graces evident in the young man and a yearning that he will not be daunted by the discouraging circumstances of Paul the prisoner. He recalls with thankfulness the faith that perpetuates a godly line from grandmother Lois through Eunice his mother, to Timothy. This faith in Christ makes a man appreciative of every gift bestowed by God and Paul refers particularly to a gift (charisma) transmitted by the laying on of his hands which he wishes Timothy to exercise diligently. For the possession of the gift is one thing: the courage and discretion to use it properly, is another. Paul is certain that the God who bestows gifts accompanies them with the moral and spiritual qualities for their exercise, "for God hath not given us the spirit of fear; but of power and of love, and of a sound mind". So, far from being put off by Paul's hardships Timothy should welcome the opportunity to participate in the affliction of the gospel as being, at the same time, an opportunity of a new experience of the power of the Gospel—specifically its death-denuding and life-giving power. The apostle indicates that his own experience runs parallel to this. He suffers: but he is not ashamed, for the God who has put him in a position of trust will sustain him in the discharge of that trust in view of the day of reckoning. Once again, therefore, Paul invites Timothy to partner him in apostolic service, bidding him "keep the pattern of sound words, which you heard from me in faith and love which is in Christ Jesus. Guard the good deposit through the Holy Spirit who abides in us".

Before attempting to elucidate some of the doctrines of the text it is worthwhile glancing at two key phrases which Paul employs, our interpretation of which will determine the exegesis of the passage as a whole.

1. "The form of sound words." The expression raises the question whether Paul refers to a stylized and more or less stereotyped form of words in which the truth was summarized or whether he refers to a more general pattern exhibiting the essentials of the truth without hardening its expression in conformity with a specific idiom. Elsewhere (1 Tim. 1:16) Paul uses the same word to describe how the extension of mercy to him as the chief of sinners constituted a pattern or form of the long-suffering of Christ to subsequent believers. All rely on the same Saviour: all are succoured by the same mercy. All give evidence of the same pattern of long-suffering on the part of Christ: but there is nothing formalised in the application of truth in each Christian's experience. We infer therefore that there is nothing in Paul's use of this expression to justify inertia or "laissez-faire" in theological thinking or practical evangelism. In the presentation of the truth we are not under obligation to retain the idiom of any age or the thought forms of any school. On the contrary, if we recognise the living quality of the truth and its essential concern with "faith and love in Jesus Christ", we lie under the necessity of giving it contemporary expression in the actual situation which confronts us. This may expose us to risk for the truth's sake. For we must be alive to the temptation to blunt the edge of truth by sheathing it in conventional forms of expression. There can be an avoidance of the relevance of truth, a shirking of the scandal of the Cross which camou-

flages itself as concern for retention of "the form of sound words", solidifying the pattern instead of recognising it as Calvin does as "a living expression of things". Our forms must not constitute an esoteric science like Egyptian hieroglyphics which are meaningful only to a few scholars. They must be the living expression of the truth which is life "in faith and love which is in Christ Jesus".

2. "That good thing committed to thee guard." Nowadays one often hears this rendered "guard the good deposit". The expression is the same as Paul uses two verses earlier where he declares confidence that God is able "to guard my deposit against that day". Whether by "my deposit" Paul means "what I have entrusted to God", or "what God has entrusted to me" will no doubt keep commentators arguing. What concerns us in the particular text before us is that the deposit entrusted to Timothy includes more than a written or oral embodiment of the gospel: includes also the gifts and graces needful to the man who is put in trust with the Gospel. As priests and levites were together responsible not only for the observance of the ritual but for the maintenance of the whole fabric of tabernacle and temple, so the Christian and especially the office-bearers of the Church have a stewardship in regard to all that affects the Church as "the pillar and ground of the truth". We have the pattern of doctrine; we have the gifts of grace. They healthily react upon one another, the appreciation of the truth stirring up the gifts of grace and grace exciting us ever more eagerly to study the pattern of sound words and this living development of grace and truth is always energized by the Spirit of God who alone can make us sufficient for the things committed to our charge.

We propose to summarize the teaching of our text in four simple propositions.

(1) Christian activity must have the Word as its constant point of reference

Paul recognizes that Timothy is and ought to be a busy man—a student and a workman. But he insists that what busies mind and hand must be consistent with, and calculated to advance, the spread and understanding of the

Gospel of Jesus Christ. The Word will provide him with his syllabus of studies and his work-sheet for life. This is a principle more easy to proclaim than to practise. For we are all disposed to develop interests and activities— legitimate in themselves but which distort the Christian order of priorities. Who of us at the end of each day can lay our hand on our heart and say "I was busy this day about my Father's business?" To be busy about the right things, to be most in the greatest matters we have to consult continually the Word of God—to consult and to obey.

Whilst we pay lip service to the supremacy of the Word in faith and life we are always under pressure to accord practical precedence to something else. Unawares, we may lay chief emphasis on a theology of experience or a theology of expedience and think that we have not deviated from the pattern of sound words. To be sure, experience colours our understanding of the Word, and expedience dictates priorities in certain limited areas; but neither of these should ever become ultimates. It is just possible that our experience is perverse or that our expedience is a cover for cowardice, avarice or vain ambition. They are themselves subject to scrutiny in the light of the Word, to correction and even to overthrow if the Word so directs.

When men take the Word of God seriously they become bold, adventurous and confident. For it is in terms of the Divine mandate that they not only covet but claim the world for Christ. Lack of physical resources, of popular acclaim, of visible evidences of success have never deterred those whose programme of activity is dictated by a conscience fully alive to the demands of the truth as it is in Christ. We are not to be like political parties having our confidence inflated or deflated by the results of opinion polls. Our task is delineated in the Word: we must examine our programmes in the light of the Word. This is our constant point of reference.

(2) The Living Christ vivifies the pattern of oral and written testimony

In advancing this proposition we have no part with those who polarize the authority of Christ and of the Scriptures.

49

In an attempt to dissipate the embarrassment which acknowledgment of the authority of Scripture involves, these people deal with the Word as though it was the product of impressionist artists. Through the mists of myth and legend they seek the figure of a real person who can speak to them with authority. We are conscious of no such disjunction between Christ and the Word His Spirit inspires. The authority of the Word is His authority.

But when we hear Paul speak "in faith and love which is in Christ Jesus" we reflect not only upon the spirit in which the apostle ministers the truth to Timothy but look to "the Author and Finisher of our faith" in whom all Christian grace has its definitive exposition and its constant inspiration. In Him, faith and love are not abstract graces or distant ideals but of the very essence of the life that is in perfect accord and fellowship with the Father. There can be no confusion in the thinking, no hesitancy or indecision in face of complex moral issues when faith and love are in perfect exercise. This is not the major part of the explanation of our Lord's knowing always the things that pleased His Father—but it is not insignificant and belongs in the area where the Christian is to be conformed to His likeness. As one who has so learned of the Lord that he reproduces his accents Paul speaks to Timothy; "In faith and love which is in Christ Jesus". He would deem himself to have failed in his ministry unless he had pointed his young friend directly to Christ himself. This is our perennial task and privilege. "We preach not ourselves but Christ Jesus the Lord." If we fail it may well be because people see too much of us and not enough of Christ in us and in our proclamation of His grace. Our graces are not on display for admiration. If our light shines and our good works are seen it is in order that men may glorify our Father who is in Heaven. We need to become more and more absorbed in the glory of our Redeemer. This is the only sure cure for undue self-consciousness; the only certain disperser of that embarrassment and shame that lurks ever in the corners of the mind. "I am not ashamed for I know whom I believed." Awareness of the living person; experience of the fellowship of Christ is what makes Paul's testimony not an official dictum but the natural and irrepressible expression of the life that is in him.

This is a first principle. There is no understanding of the Scriptures; there is no reception of testimony until the reader and the hearer become aware of the living Person of the Saviour whom it all concerns. At whatever Scripture we begin we must preach to our people Christ. He is the meaning of it all.

The worthy proclaiming of the Saviour involves us in the faith and love of which He is Author and Finisher. We cannot genuinely invite men to trust in a Saviour in whom we do not ourselves confide. We cannot hold up to admiration love which in our own hearts goes unrequited. The elucidation of Biblical doctrine is never an exclusively intellectual exercise aimed at formal correctness of notions— but always a stimulation of the heart's affections. What the systematizing of doctrine does is to assemble the information we have about our Lord and His work, so that our devotion to His Person will be more intense and intelligent. "Whom having not seen we love." We do not love the unknown; we need to know more about Him that we may love Him better. This is our involvement "in faith and love which is in Christ Jesus". It is not a matter of mere formal correctness of concept and practice but of personal enthusiasm for Him who loved us and gave Himself for us. We move in the same area of thought where the apostle speaks of "faith and a good conscience". They go together—the proclamation and practice of godliness. Would God that we all could say without blushing that our testimony is "in faith and love which is in Christ Jesus".

(3) **What God gives the Christian must guard**

"Guard the good deposit," said Paul, as one who had himself a lively sense of stewardship in regard to the Gospel of Jesus Christ. But here we have the paradox of Christian experience so well expressed in the proverb. "There is that scattereth and yet increaseth; and there is that withholdeth more than is meet but it tendeth to poverty" (Prov. 2:24). For the guarding of the gospel and its graces is not by incarceration. He who hides his talent in the earth and says

51

to His master "Lo there thou hast that is thine" has opted out of his stewardship and invites the description "thou wicked and slothful servant . . ." The guarding of the gospel necessitates the proclamation of the Gospel in its fulness and purity by word and life. It is not by accident but as one carried on by the essential logic of the truth, that Paul, warning against "the sleight of men and cunning craftiness, whereby they lie in wait to deceive", sets over against this "speaking the truth in love". The truth is not guarded by silence but by proclamation in love. In the constant human debate we must therefore be in the thick of things, making known the Gospel of salvation. By all means let us test every formulation of doctrine by reference to the Word. Let us try every spirit whether it be of God. Let us not yield one jot or tittle of God's revealed truth. But let us remember that we are holders not of a treasure which is to be hidden in the dark vaults of theological banks, but of the minted currency of the kingdom of God which is for use, for the enrichment of all who receive it. "Stir up the gift that is in thee . . . and so guard the good deposit."

(4) Christian guardianship can be discharged only in the power of the Holy Spirit

"Guard through the Holy Spirit" is Paul's counsel and it confirms what we have said of the implicate of applying the truth to the existent situation. For the Spirit of God is not the spirit of inertia but of power. His living energy is the life of the Christian and the Church. He it is who leads us into the truth, who teaches us the things of Christ. If in our hearts there is the glow of love to Christ; if zeal for His glory burns in us, be sure it is by the working in us of the Spirit promised by the Saviour—the Holy Paraclete of whom He declared—"He shall not speak of Himself; but whatsoever He shall hear that shall he speak. . . . He shall glorify me for he shall receive of mine and shall show it unto you." Not to one unwilling and aloof do we cry "Come, Holy Spirit, our souls inspire . . ." but to one who was given to the Church at Pentecost to be in her for ever. So Peter proclaimed, "This Jesus hath God raised up. . . . Therefore being by the right hand of God exalted and having received

52

of the Father the promise of the Holy Ghost, he hath shed forth this which ye now see and hear." This was the power for which the apostles were bidden tarry at Jerusalem. This is the power which is the continuing gift to the Church. "He dwells in us," says Paul. Elsewhere he reminds us that our bodies are the temple of the Spirit of God. This is what assures us that the Christian gospel is not the proclamation of an unattainable ideal. There is a communication of power: and in the guarding of the truth we do not go it alone. He who makes the truth "spirit and life" is with us and in us. Let us seek an intensifying awareness of His presence and power. So let us "guard the good deposit". May His blessing abide upon us.

C. GRAHAM

A FAITHFUL SAYING

"This is a faithful saying, and worthy of all acceptation, that Christ Jesus came into the world to save sinners; of whom I am chief."

I TIM. I :I5

This is the first of the five "faithful sayings" in the Pastoral Epistles with which Paul confronts us. It was not a new saying, but one which was embodied in the doctrine and life of the early Christian Church. Its importance lies in its substance which is the treatment of sin and salvation, and for that reason it merits our attention. Sin is our basic problem in life and it is essential that we understand its implications and how to be saved from its consequences. We can do so by turning to our Bibles with confidence to learn from God what the way of salvation is.

(1) The fact of sin

In acts of gross misbehaviour we readily recognize sin, but we make a serious mistake if our view of it does not go beyond that. In the text, Paul speaks about a world of sinners and calls himself the very worst of them. Did he mean that before his conversion on the Damascus Road he had lived a thoroughly bad life and now viewed his past with shame? Is that what Paul means when he describes himself as the chief of sinners? Surely not, for even before his conversion to Christ he was a deeply religious man who could bear favourable comparison with the most devout of his day. He could confidently boast, as he does in his letter to the Philippians, "If any other man thinketh that he hath whereof he might trust in the flesh, I more: circumcised the eighth day, of the stock of Israel, of the tribe of Benjamin, an Hebrew of the Hebrews; as touching the law, a Pharisee; concerning zeal, persecuting the Church: touching the righteousness which is in the law, blameless" (Phil. 3:4-6).

Here we have a devout Jew, who in the eyes of his fellow countrymen lived a life beyond reproach, and yet now he confesses himself to be the chief of sinners. When we ask why this man should make such a confession, we are led to see that sin goes much deeper than we think.

In His Word, God never allows us to forget the consequences and condemnation of sin. Irreparable damage to the spiritual life of man was caused by the disobedience of our first parents during their probation in the Garden of Eden. And all the generations from Adam to our own have inherited a sinful bias which is part of our nature. We have been, as David puts it, "shapen in iniquity and conceived in sin" (Ps. 51:5). "The imagination of man's heart," says God, "is evil from his youth" (Gen. 8:21). The Bible knows nothing of universal human goodness. "The Lord looked down from heaven upon the children of men, to see if there were any that did understand, and seek God. They are all gone aside, they are all together become filthy: there is none that doeth good, no, not one" (Ps. 14:2–3). What the Prophet Isaiah affirms is startlingly true; "All we like sheep have gone astray; we have turned every one to his own way" (Isa. 53:6). God is holy and He does not and cannot allow us to regard sin with indifference. From the beginning of their history, the Israelites were taught how offensive it was to Him. The System of Substitutionary Sacrifice presented a grim picture indeed; the flaying of the sacrifice and its final destruction by fire served to remind them of what sin deserved. The burden of the prophetic message throughout the Old Testament dispensation was the declaration of God's righteous anger against a sinning people.

In the New Testament we discover the same serious view of sin. The Lord Jesus doesn't tell us that basically man is good and noble and that given proper conditions he will reveal human goodness. No, He tells us that basically the nature of man is corrupt and twisted. It is He who gives us the most striking analysis of the human heart. "For from within, out of the heart of men, proceed evil thoughts, adulteries, fornications, murders, thefts, covetousness, wickedness, deceit, lasciviousness, an evil eye, blasphemy,

55

pride, foolishness: all these evil things come from within, and defile the man" (Mark 7:21-23). Now if we examine ourselves in the light of this analysis we will see how far short we come of God's Holy Standard. Perhaps we may be able to pride ourselves that our moral rectitude has prevented us from outward impropriety. But is that sufficient for us to pass the scrutiny of a Holy and Omniscient God? When we go back to the Bible, it reveals that the sweep of God's commandments goes beyond mere conformity to the letter of the law. What God requires is that the disposition of our being should live within the spirit of the law. By way of illustration, let us consider the sixth and seventh commandments, and see if we live within the spirit of them. The sixth commandment is, "Thou shalt not kill." The Word of God, however, says elsewhere, "Whosoever hateth his brother is a murderer: and ye know that no murderer hath eternal life abiding in him" (1 John 3:15). So that not only is murder a sin, but hating a man is the same sin in germ. The seventh commandment forbids adultery. But Jesus elaborates that and says, "Whosoever looketh on a woman to lust after her hath committed adultery with her already in his heart" (Matt. 5:28). The prohibition in the commandment is not only uncleanness of life but uncleanness of thought as well. If we examine our lives carefully in the light of the commandments, we shall see how far short we come of the standard of God. It is one thing to claim that we have conformed to the letter of the law, but it is quite another thing to live within the spirit of it. "The Lord seeth not as man seeth; for man looketh on the outward appearance, but the Lord looketh on the heart" (1 Sam. 16:7).

We must also remember the power of sin which renders us incapable of reforming ourselves Godwards. Until we are converted we are children of wrath, children of disobedience, or to use another Biblical expression, slaves of sin. When we consider the tyranny that sin exercises over us, we can understand the heart cry of the Apostle, when he expressed his sense of frustration that sin should still inhere in his life as a Christian: "For I know that in me (that is, in my flesh) dwelleth no good thing: for to will is present with me;

56

but how to perform that which is good I find not. For the good that I would I do not: but the evil which I would not, that I do. O wretched man that I am! who shall deliver me from the body of this death?" (Rom. 7:18–19, 24). Our plight is serious, and we see how serious it is when we consider God's inexorable sentence passed upon sin. God can no more wink at sin than an earthly judge can wink at crimes against the civil law, and His sentence is death— "the wages of sin is death" (Rom. 6:23).

Now, however revolting physical death is to us, that in itself is not the most alarming aspect in the punishment of sin. What must alarm us is that after death there is the Judgment. "For we must all appear before the judgment seat of Christ; that every one may receive the things done in his body, according to that he hath done, whether it be good or bad" (2 Cor. 5:10). It may be asked what will happen to us if we appear before that heavenly tribunal in an unsaved condition bearing with us our sins of thought, and word, and deed? It will mean being sentenced to eternal separation from God and Jesus draws the veil of the unseen world aside in order that we may see what that involves. To be separated from God is to be cast into outer darkness, where, as Jesus says, in the abyssmal depths of hell there is "weeping and gnashing of teeth" (Matt. 8:12). Well might we be filled with forebodings with regard to life beyond death. But we can be thankful to God for this faithful saying which is the very essence of the Gospel, "that Christ Jesus came into the world to save sinners".

(2) The sinner's Saviour

Paul is speaking about a world of sinners into which Christ Jesus entered in order to save from sin's power and desert.

If we ask, "who is Jesus Christ?" He, Himself answers our question. "For I came down from heaven, not to do mine own will, but the will of Him that sent me" (John 6:38). In His great priestly intercession before His death on the Cross Jesus prayed, "And now, O Father, glorify thou me with thine own self with the glory which I had with thee before the world was" (John 17:5). These portions of

Scripture reveal that the Lord Jesus had a pre-existent state in heaven before His human life began on earth. He was the Divine Son of God—co-equal and co-eternal with the Father. And from that state of Glory He came forth to be a Saviour.

> He came down to earth from heaven,
> who is God and Lord of all.
>
> C. F. ALEXANDER

The question may be raised, can His claim to such unique heavenly origin be substantiated? To answer that we need only point to His unblameable life, His divine teaching, and His supernatural power.

When we consider the humiliation involved in Christ coming to our earth, we can understand the wonder of the Apostle when he wrote to the Corinthians; "For ye know the grace of our Lord Jesus Christ, that though he was rich, yet for your sakes he became poor, that ye through his poverty might be rich" (2 Cor. 8:9). The thought of it never ceased to overwhelm Paul that He who was in the form of God and thought it not robbery to be equal with Him, "made himself of no reputation, and took upon him the form of a servant, and was made in the likeness of men: and being found in fashion as a man, he humbled himself, and became obedient unto death, even the death of the Cross" (Phil. 2:6–8). In order to provide salvation for His people the Eternal Son became an infant of days. "When the fulness of the time was come, God sent forth His Son, made of a woman, made under the law, to redeem them that were under the law, that we might receive the adoption of sons" (Gal. 4:4–5).

To understand fully how Christ Jesus saves from sin, we must consider the operation of God's Grace in Old Testament times. In the law of sacrifice, the Israelites were made to see that the requirements of God's Law had to be met in full. "Life shall go for life, eye for eye, tooth for tooth, hand for hand, foot for foot" (Deut. 19:21). If the life of the penitent was not to be forfeited for his sin, the penalty of that sin had to be inflicted upon the substitutionary sacrifice. "For the life of the flesh is in the blood," says God, "and I have given it to you upon the altar to make an atonement for your souls: for it is the blood that maketh an atonement for the soul" (Lev. 17:11). The blood of the sacrifice was given in the place of the offender—life was given for life. But these animal sacrifices themselves had no saving merit: they were only a ceremonial expedient for the present until the time came when God's Son offered himself as a living sacrifice in the place of the guilty. Christ Jesus came to be a Saviour: He came from heaven to be both Priest and Sacrifice and to offer Himself up to God, once and for all, for the sins of His people. John the Baptist describes Him as "the Lamb of God, which taketh away the sin of the world" (John 1:29).

> Not all the blood of beasts on Jewish altars slain,
> Could give the guilty conscience peace or wash away the stain.
> But Christ, the heavenly Lamb, takes all our sins away;
> A sacrifice of nobler name and richer blood, than they.
>
> ISAAC WATTS

Jesus' death upon the Cross was not a martyr's death. It was a transaction in which the Father inflicted upon the Son the just punishment for sin. In his sermon at Pentecost, Peter says that although Jesus was taken by wicked hands and crucified, yet He was delivered over to that death by the determinate counsel and foreknowledge of God. Far from being a passive onlooker at the Cross, God had planned this atonement and was actively engaged in the infliction of sufferings upon His Son. "It pleased the Lord to bruise him; he hath put him to grief" (Isa. 53:10). And the bruising and grief borne by Christ was not for any sin that He had done but for the sins of others. If it be asked, "was there another way whereby God could save the guilty from their sin?"—the answer must be no. Had there been another way would God ever have sent His Son to the death of the Cross? This was the only way in which His righteous law could be upheld and vindicated, and sinners escape the just condemnation of sin.

At the Cross we see the depths to which Christ Jesus descended in order to save from sin: for He went to the depths of hell. His manhood was perfect and therefore His physical sufferings were the most acute that could be endured. But we must never forget the indefinable intensity of His spiritual sufferings. On one occasion, Dr. John Duncan, the remarkable 19th century Free Church Professor of Hebrew in New College, Edinburgh, was lecturing to his students and referring the words of Psalm 22 verse 1, "My God, my God, why hast thou forsaken me", to the sufferings of Christ. He asked his students, "D'ye know what it was—dying on the Cross, forsaken by His Father?—It was damnation—and damnation taken lovingly". Christ Jesus can well call our attention to His sufferings in the words of the prophet when he describes Jerusalem in the day of her desolating judgment. "Is it nothing to you, all ye that pass by? behold, and see if there be any sorrow like unto my sorrow, which is done unto me, wherewith the Lord hath afflicted me in the day of his fierce anger" (Lam. 1:12). It took "the bloody sweat of Gethsemane, and the unfathomable agony of Calvary to atone for sin", and that is why we may never treat it lightly nor take salvation for granted.

There comes a time in the year when businesses do stock-taking. They review the present in the light of the past and assess their profit or loss. If we do some spiritual stock-taking we shall see how far short of the glory of God we come, and how deeply involved in sin we are. What then are we to do? When the jailer at Philippi came under conviction his cry of distress was, "What must I do to be saved?" And what he was asked to do is what we must all do, "Believe on the Lord Jesus Christ, and thou shalt be saved" (Acts 16:30–31). Because of the infinite worth of the person of Christ and because of the infinite merit of His finished work, "He is able to save to the uttermost all who come unto God by Him" (Heb. 7:25), so that even the chief of sinners will find that Christ is indeed an adequate Saviour.

"This is a faithful saying, and worthy of all acceptation, that Christ Jesus came into the world to save sinners; of whom I am chief."

Nothing either great or small—
Nothing, sinner no;
Jesus died and did it all,
Long, long, ago.

"It is finished", yes, indeed,
    Finished every jot.
Sinner, this is all you need,
    Tell me, is it not?

Weary, working, burdened one,
Wherefore toil you so?
Cease your doing, all was done,
    Long, long, ago.

Cast your deadly doing down,
    Down at Jesus' feet;
Stand in him, in him alone,
    Gloriously complete.

H. FERRIER

THE BURNING BUSH

". . . the bush burned with fire, and the bush was not consumed."
(EXOD. 3:2)

This familiar incident which has become the badge of Presbyterianism throughout the world blends in a beautiful way the natural with the supernatural. The bush was probably an ordinary bramble bush which, as Dean Stanley says, was the most characteristic kind of vegetation in those parts. But the ordinary became extraordinary, for the bramble bush became the sanctuary of the living God. That part of the Sinai desert became "holy ground" and was pronounced so by God Himself.

Like Moses we too are interested in this burning bush for God was in it and from it revealed Himself to His Church as the living God. But like Moses we need to turn aside to see and to hear. And as we do we are immediately faced with:

(1) A mystery that astonishes us

It astonished Moses who was attending to his regular duties as a shepherd in the area of the mountainous range of Horeb. "I will turn aside and see this great sight." This was no ordinary sight for this was no ordinary bush fire. Its significance reached down through the centuries. Moses when he was blessing the Tribes Joseph entreated for him the "goodwill of Him that dwelt in the bush" (Deut. 33:16). Jesus when discussing with the Sadducees the resurrection of the dead referred them to this incident (Luke 20:37). And Stephen in his able defence before the Council recounted this phenomenon as an integral part of Old Testament history and a turning point in the personal history of Moses (Acts 7:30-34).

The first astonishing thing about the whole incident was

of course that *the bush which burned did not burn out.* This, needless to say, had nothing to do with the bush itself. It could have been any bush. Nor was it astonishing that the bush was on fire. This could happen in our own country through the heat of the sun. The amazing thing was that the bush was not consumed. Although the nature of fire is to devour and burn up it was incapable of doing so in this instance. It was precisely this inability of the fire to devour the bush that constituted the mystery. The scene was therefore not in the realm of the natural but the supernatural. It lay outside the normal and entered the supernormal. And this immediately plummets us into the realm of mystery. The supernatural is above us and beyond us, and we can only stand and stare.

That this is so was the unqualified admission of Paul who said, "This is a great mystery", when he was dealing with the supernatural relationship between Christ and His Church (Eph. 5:32). Similarly, in speaking of the supernatural nature of the resurrection of the body at the return of Christ he acknowledged, "Behold I show you a mystery . . ." (1 Cor. 15:51).

The second astonishing thing was that *the Lord was in the bush* (Exod. 3:4) and that God who is a consuming fire did not see fit to consume it. Indeed He saw fit not to consume it for our instruction and comfort.

But how could the glorious and mighty Lord be in a bush? And how could He be there in the form of fire? The mystery here is not of God manifest in flesh but in fire and flame. This of course is matched by the mystery of Pentecost when God the Holy Spirit appeared as cloven tongues like as of fire. But this present appearance of God to Moses was not the only appearance of God to man before the incarnation. There were several theophanies and each was clothed in mystery, as this one was.

How good it is that we do not have to solve the mystery before we can believe it. How good too that we do not have to solve the greatest mystery of all before being blessed through it—"And without controversy great is the mystery of godliness, God manifest in the flesh" (1 Tim. 3:16). Let us therefore bow reverently before the mystery here as

Moses did and decline to intrude where angels fear to tread.

But not only are we faced with a mystery that astonishes us but also with,

(2) An emblem that instructs us

Unquestionably the mysterious is meant to be instructive. And while it is no one's province to attempt an analysis of the bush and the fire (which is to miss the whole point) it is in everyone's wisdom to hear what God is saying to us out of the bush and to be taught by Him.

Two lessons may be noted here. It is first an emblem of *the existence of the Church*. This bush was not burning in the land of Canaan, a pleasant land flowing with milk and honey, but in the arid Sinai wilderness. And so is the Church. The bush represents the Church in the wilderness and not yet in glory. The Church commenced in the wilderness—in a world that knew not God—and will continue there until Christ, at His coming, will take His people home. Likewise all who through grace are members of the Church live in a desert situation and are strangers and pilgrims in it. They are in a world that has deserted God (and is therefore "desert") and upon which the wrath of God rests.

But the bush burning so brightly and unremittingly was not a tall stately cedar rising majestically above the common vegetation of the wilderness. It was just a humble bramble bush that kept very close to mother earth and had no aspirations of grandeur.

Now this is quite significant for it reinforces the image of the Church spelt out for us by St. Paul in writing to the Corinthian Church. The Church is composed of "not many wise men . . . mighty . . . noble". Indeed God has seen fit to choose "the foolish things, the weak, the base (or the insignificant), the despised, the things that are not to bring to nought things that are."

How alien to this description of the composition of the Church is, for example, the pomp and pomposity of some of its communions! Its copes and mitres, its professional musicians, its impressive ceremonial can find no support in Apostolic Christianity. How alien to the simplicity that is in Christ! How proper, on the other hand, that humility and simplicity should adorn the church and its ministry in all ages.

But this bush growing in the wilderness and lowly in its kind was a bush on fire. And while the indwelling presence of God shone from the bush with glory and majesty (for the glory of His presence could not be hidden), nevertheless the fire was the symbol of something quite different. It was surely emblematic of "the affliction of my people which are in Egypt" (Exod. 3:7, Acts 7:34). The flames that unsuccessfully licked the bush in the wilderness signified the persecution to which the people of God were being subjected in Egypt by a tyrannical Pharaoh. And the cry of a persecuted people came to the ears of the Lord of Sabbaoth who raised up Moses and called him to be His people's liberator at the bush which was not consumed.

But the emblem is instructive not only in its looking back to Israel oppressed in Egypt but in looking forward to the Church persecuted by the world. Down through the ages the glorious body of Christ has been persecuted. Through the wilderness there moves a persecuted and an afflicted people. Fire has ever followed the Church of God on its way to the beautiful city of God. Singeing and burning have ever been the Church's experience as it presses on to God, and so it will be till the Church militant becomes the Church triumphant.

But we have not yet reached the pith of the lesson. The bush not only represents the existence of the Church but *the continuing existence of the Church.* "The bush was not consumed."

The Church which God built on the rock is a Church against which the gates of hell shall not prevail. It is resistant to the flames and fires of persecution. It increases in the fire and is perpetuated in the devouring flame. The testimony of church history is eloquent on this and confirms the apostolic observation in 2 Cor. 4:8, 9. "Troubled on every side yet not distressed . . . perplexed but not in despair, persecuted but not forsaken, cast down but not destroyed". It is utterly impossible for this to happen for God has promised to present it to Himself a glorious Church (conformed to the glorious humanity of the Son of

God), and free from spot, or wrinkle, or any such thing—
faultless and perfect, holy and blameless (Eph. 5:25 et seq.).

> Glorious things of thee are spoken
> Zion, city of our God!
> He whose word cannot be broken
> Formed thee for His own abode.
> On the Rock of Ages founded,
> What can shake thy sure repose?
> With Salvation's walls surrounded,
> Thou mayst smile at all thy foes.

The unalterable purpose of God will yet be fulfilled in the
unutterable delight of the Church. It cannot be otherwise
for "God is in the midst of her; she shall not be moved"
(Ps. 46:5).

But this Church of which the burning bush is an emblem
is made up of individuals. The body of Christ has many
members and what is true of the body is true of the individual member. David's clear testimony was, "Thou shalt
guide me with Thy counsel, and afterward receive me to
glory" (Ps. 73:24). If we belong to the Lord and are under
His guidance and tutelage it cannot but be that "afterward" we shall be received into glory. Jesus is very explicit,
"Whosoever believeth in Him should not perish but have
everlasting life" (John 3:16).

Let us take another look at the bush? In doing so we
are faced not only with a mystery that astonishes us and
with an emblem that instructs us, but with,

(3) A magnet that attracts us

It attracted Moses.

First *it turned him aside* (Exod. 3:3). He could not go
on. He had to go over to "see this great sight". Even before
he heard the voice of God he had to admit that it was a
"great sight". And little did he think as he approached the
bush that defied the flames that he was to stand in the
presence of the living God. God, the God of glory, the
"I am that I am" was there, and every sight of such a God
is a great sight, for it was a great God who was there.

The Church where God is obviously and truly present is
a great sight because there is life there. His glory can be

66

seen and His voice can be heard, and this is what attracts the attention of men in every age. Those who esteem the reproach of Christ greater riches than the treasures in Egypt are attracted to the place where His honour dwells. A Church that is dead and lifeless may attract dead and lifeless people, but it has no attraction for the people of God. One of the evidences of spiritual life within us is our desire to stand in God's presence on God's day and be rid as far as possible of the pressures and other concomitants of a world such as ours. Men and women with the faith of Moses are turned aside with the prayer of David,

> That I thy power may behold,
> and brightness of thy face,
> As I have seen thee heretofore
> within thy holy place.

The magnet unquestionably is "God in the midst". And when we turn aside it is to see no man but Jesus only.

But it not only turned him aside. It also *led him to worship* (Exod. 3:-6). The place was pronounced "holy ground". The bush became a sanctuary. And approaching as near as he dared, "Moses hid his face; for he was afraid to look upon God". That is worship. It is a basic characteristic of true worship to get down at His feet. By all means let us sing unto the Lord: let us make a joyful noise unto the rock of our salvation". But also "let us worship and bow down: let us kneel before the Lord our maker" (Ps. 95:1–2). By all means let us come to the throne of grace boldly; but with a boldness that is consecrated by reverence for the One who sits upon the throne. As long as unholy people like ourselves are on holy ground our boldness will take us as far as the footstool of His throne and that is as far as we need or dare approach.

Let us be watchful therefore that our worship has in it something of this hiding of the face, something of the consciousness of being in the presence of the living God Who is glorious in holiness. And let us never confuse spiritual worship with mere noise, fussy activity or outward display; for true worship is marked by reverence, humility and adoration in the presence of God. "Moses hid his face; for he was afraid to look upon God."

I do not ask you, who read these words, to what Church you belong. But I do ask if you belong to the God Who dwelt in the bush, before Whom Moses bowed. This is of supreme importance. If you believe in the Lord Jesus Christ, then you belong to His Church, and to a people whom He will never forsake, but will yet translate from the wilderness to that region where grows the "tree of life which is in the midst of the paradise of God".

A. G. Ross

HAPPINESS

"Rejoice, and be exceeding glad . . ."
MATT. 5:12

Each first of January we wish each other a Happy New Year. In spite of the inauspicious auguries for the fulfilment of the wish the greeting is not wrong or misplaced. The desire for happiness is an inbuilt aspiration of the human heart; we would go further and say that it is a God-implanted desire. It certainly is a perennial pursuit of the heart of man. It is also an ultimate of salvation for the consummation of redemption will witness the redeemed of God made "perfectly blessed in the full enjoying of God throughout eternity".

Contrary to popular belief the Christian religion is not anti-joy. This is a warped misconception fostered by a lying devil. The Bible certainly denounces and warns against the so-called pleasures of sin, but the religion it teaches is not kill-joy. There is nothing sour or ascetic about it. True, it has a place for the bitter-herbs with the paschal meal; it inculcates the godly sorrow of repentance, it speaks of taking up the Cross and following Christ, but the bitter-herbs are not the whole meal. The roast lamb of the Passover is the main part of the feast. The Christian life is a feast and not a fast. The Gospel is good news—not heavy tidings. There are "pleasures forevermore" at God's right hand; "in His presence there is fullness of joy" (Ps. 16:11). Happiness, or blessedness (the words are interchangeable) is of the very essence of the Christian religion. Rejoicing is a continual exercise of the Christian life. "Rejoice in the Lord alway; and again I say Rejoice" (Phil. 4:4).

(1) Happiness is a by-product

Yet in a very real sense happiness is a by-product of life.

69

If we make it our main goal it often eludes us as the rainbow's end recedes from the little boy who fondly seeks the legendary pot of gold! Though one of the main assets of the religious life, happiness itself is a by-product of duty and service, of righteousness and holiness. Those who see it independently of duty and service to God will find nothing but disillusionment and discontent in the long run. Like Moses' shining face, a by-product of his fellowship with God on the Mount, happiness is given often as an unexpected bonus to faith and service. Wordsworth uses the phrase in one of his poems, "surprised by joy", which C. S. Lewis aptly took as the title of his autobiography.

There are various recipes for happiness. They may be graded according to age. The child finds happiness (at least for a short time) in his toys, goodies, and sweetmeats. Youth finds it in fun and excitement, seeks it in sex, the dance-floor or discotheque. The man, in a well-paid secure job, in a home, in hobbies. Age? There is not much in the way of creature-happiness that age can look forward to with its limitations, physical and sometimes mental. There was a good deal of sound and sober wisdom in Barzillai's courteous refusal of king David's offer of a place at court. "I am this day four-score years old: and can I discern between good and evil? can thy servant taste what I eat and what I drink? Can I hear anymore the voice of singing men and singing women? Wherefore then should thy servant be yet a burden to my lord the king?" (2 Sam. 19:35).

Obviously we must look elsewhere for the ingredients of true and lasting happiness. These recipes for blessedness have an ingredient missing, or rather they are the wrong ingredients. These kinds of joy may give temporary satisfaction. They may divert but can never truly satisfy. There is an ingredient missing and it is the divine. God is left out of account and there cannot be any true happiness without God.

(2) The divine recipe

Scripture gives guidance here. Happiness, or blessedness, begins with God. One of Augustine's prayers in his famous "*Confessions*" is quoted until it should have become threadbare were it not for its intrinsic truth, "O Lord, our hearts

were made for Thee and they are restless until they find
their rest in Thee". No man, woman or child is happy,
truly happy, who is leaving God out, who has no room for
Christ in the house of his soul. Israel of old were pronounced
happy because they were a people "saved by the Lord"
(Deut. 33:29). Jehovah God was in their midst.

(3) Happiness founded on reconciliation to God

For sinful man one of the main ingredients in happiness
is forgiveness. No man can be happy who is not at peace
with God. An honest man who has unfortunately fallen
into debt is miserable until that debt is cleared. We cannot
be happy and be debtors to the Law of God, hopelessly,
head-over-heels in debt! So the Psalmist exclaimed,
"Blessed is he whose transgression is forgiven, whose sin is
covered. Blessed is the man unto whom the Lord imputeth
not iniquity . . ." (Ps. 32:1). John Bunyan, in his own
picturesque way, gives expression to this when he tells how
his pilgrim lost his burden. The heavy, galling load, the
source of all Christian's misery, unstrapped itself when the
pilgrim came to the place where was a cross and a man
hanging there—the Cross and the Man—and it rolled
away out of sight into an empty tomb. A brilliant stroke of
evangelical genius! In two or three sentences Bunyan sums
up the theological truth that Christ died for our sins
according to the Scriptures and that He rose again (the
empty tomb) for our justification. Little wonder the freed
Pilgrim gave three leaps for joy and sang,

> Bless'd Cross! Bless'd Sepulchre! bless'd rather be
> The man that there was put to shame for me.

For the sinner happiness begins with forgiveness. And
not just pardon but justification. The pardoned man has
his debt cancelled but he remains poor; he has not a penny
to his name. The justified sinner is, by way of imputed
righteousness, a millionaire! He has Christ's untold riches
of righteousness laid to his account. He can never be poor
again. To quote Bunyan, in another connection, though on a
similar theme, "'Twas glorious to me to see His exaltation
and the worth and prevalency of all His benefits, and that

because now I could look from myself to Him and should reckon, that all those graces of God that now were given to me, were yet but like those cracked groats and four-pence-halfpennies that rich men carry in their purses, when their gold is in their trunks at home! Oh! I saw that my gold was in my trunk at home! In Christ my Lord and Saviour. Now Christ was all; all my wisdom, all my righteousness, all my satisfaction, and all my redemption". *Christ all my righteousness.* It makes for happiness.

(4) Happiness linked with unselfishness

Another indispensable ingredient in true happiness is unselfishness. This is rather a negative way of expressing it, but then we live in rather a negative world. The positive virtue, or course, is love. No man devoid of love can hope to be truly happy. The selfish man has an insatiable appetite to cater for, like the sea, the grave and the barren womb, selfishness can never say, "Enough". Selfishness eats up happiness: it is self-consuming in a horribly cannaba-listic way! But love does not think of itself; it thinks of others, it serves others, it suffers for others. And happiness come to it by way of bonus! Our exemplar in this, as in so many things, is the Lord Jesus Himself. A man of sorrows yet, paradoxically, He could not be termed unhappy. It was His joy to do the Father's will and to save His people according to that will. He loved the Father, He loved His own in the world and Jesus knew what true happiness was. So may we if we follow His steps and fulfil His new commandment to love one another.

(5) Happiness dependent on consistent Christian living

Again, happiness is linked with the consistency of a Christian life. The first Psalm makes this clear. "Blessed (or happy) is the man who walks not in the counsel of the wicked . . . but his delight is in the law of the Lord . . ." (Ps. 1:1–2). For if we are not saved by our keeping of the law, we are certainly saved to keep God's holy law. "Freed from the law, O happy condition!" was never meant to be construed as a pre-requisite for happiness, for blessedness is to be found by those who "walk in the way of the Lord to all well-pleasing". To stray out of the way is to court unhappiness. In spite of the ease of Bye-Path Meadow to pilgrim feet in comparison with the King's Highway, it eventually leads to Doubting Castle and the dungeon of Giant Despair. David found this out when he sinned grievously over Uriah's wife and for a time lost the joy of salvation. Without fearfulness but in the fear of the Lord we must look to our ways and watch our conduct if we would know the sunny side of the Christian footpath. We have constantly need of this prayer:

> Hold up my goings, Lord, me guide
> in those Thy paths divine,
> So that my footsteps may not slide
> out of those ways of Thine.

PS. 17:5

(6) Happiness and the Cross of Salvation

The last ingredients in true happiness we would mention are, at first sight, surprising, even paradoxical. The characteristics of the happy man are set forth by our Lord in the opening of His great address to His disciples, the Sermon on the Mount. There He declares that the blessed, or happy, people are the mourners, the poor, the hungry, the persecuted, the meek. These rather seem to militate against joy and gladness: they appear rather as intruders into happiness. Not so! They give flavour to the meal like salt and vinegar. True, by themselves they do not make a meal, but they give taste and quality to it, as the bitter-herbs to the paschal meal. So Jesus says, ". . . Blessed are the meek . . . blessed are those that are persecuted for righteousness sake. Rejoice and be exceeding glad . . . !" (Matt. 5: 3, 4, 5, 10, 12). Such knowledge may be too strange for us, too high to understand. Yet it was exemplified in the early Christians persecuted for the Gospel's sake. They returned out of prison to their fellow-believers rejoicing that they were counted worthy to suffer for the name of Jesus. Paul and Silas not only prayed but sang praises as they sat with bleeding backs and their feet fast in the stocks. Little wonder Luke records that the "prisoners heard them"

73

(Acts 16:25). Heard them with astonishment. But they were merely repeating the experience of the Man of Sorrows Himself (though not in any penal, expiatory way) who is also the Man of Joy. And so the Christian believer learns to "glory in infirmities" (2 Cor. 12:9), to "glory in tribulations also" (Rom. 5:3). He knows the secret which grace alone can teach to be "exceeding joyful *in* all his tribulations", not after they are all over. But if the Christian believer knows the secret of joy in the midst of troubles what will the joy be when they are all past!

Happiness? Not an impossibility even in a world in which "man is born to trouble as the sparks fly upward" (Job 5:7), rather a reality for those who are in Christ reconciled to God by His blood, stayed by His grace, for all who live by faith in Christ Jesus and are obedient to the heavenly vision.

J. W. Fraser

THE GRACE THAT BRINGS
SALVATION

"Who, when he came, and had seen the grace of God, was glad, and exhorted them all, that with purpose of heart they would cleave unto the Lord."
ACTS 11:23

It has often happened in the history of the Church that what was designed to bring about its destruction, was, under God's hand, instrumental in its expansion. By the persecutions which followed the death of Stephen many of the disciples were driven out of Palestine. Some made their way to Cyprus and other islands of the Levant, while others went as far as Antioch, the capital of Syria. Although those disciples could be banished they could not be silenced. In Antioch, some Greek-speaking Jews proclaimed the Word not only to their fellow-Jews, but also to the Gentiles. The question of whether the Gospel ought to be preached to the Gentiles was one to which the Jews had for long given but one answer, an answer born of the spirit of exclusivism and national prejudice that had held sway among them for generations. However, God's blessing followed the preaching of the Gospel in Antioch, and many were converted, fully justifying the boldness and the zeal of those who had not hesitated to preach to the Gentiles the Lord Jesus.

It is not surprising that the news of the revival in Antioch excited interest among the disciples in Jerusalem, and they resolved to send someone to Antioch to find out at first hand what was actually taking place, and to give such help as the situation there might require. For this mission, they chose Barnabas, a person well-fitted for such an undertaking. A Hellenistic Jew, a native of Cyprus, he was a spiritually-minded man of sound judgment, who could be relied upon to give a just appraisal of the situation.

It is interesting to learn from the words of our text his recognition of what was actually happening in the Syrian capital, and we might first of all consider:

(1) What he saw on arrival there

He saw the grace of God. There is no word about his seeing or hearing things that cut across the early prejudices and traditions of the Jews. There is no word of his seeing what many of his fellow-Jews would have deemed irregular, or even offensive. He saw right to the root cause of all that was taking place where the Gospel was proclaimed; he saw—the grace of God.

This was a clear-cut answer to the problem that had given rise to a number of questions in those early days of the Church. God had set the seal of His approval upon this ministry to the Gentiles, and vindicated the actions of those who would make known to all the world the unsearchable riches of Christ. Moreover, this is a glorious description of what underlay the change in men's lives that was so obvious to Barnabas when he arrived there.

It is evident that Jews and Gentiles in that region had believed in the Lord. And it must be remembered that however many privileges those Jews had previously enjoyed, and however much the Gentiles may have lacked them, nothing less than the grace of God could turn the hearts of men of either class to the Lord; while, on the other hand, that same grace was sufficient to convert as many as were made partakers of it.

If the blessings of which the fruits were seen in Antioch are traced to their source, we find that it is all of grace! The election of those predestinated unto eternal life is called the "election of grace". It is not because of anything foreseen in those who are to be the subjects of that grace, but according to the sovereign purpose of a gracious God, who loved His people with an everlasting love. The very heart of the revelation God has given of Himself speaks to us of grace—full and sovereign and free, and the Son's giving of Himself to suffer and die for sinners is the exercise of His grace.

In the lives of those converts grace is seen in its irresistible

76

power. Those who had been enemies of the Cross of Christ, whether consciously and avowedly, or in the darkness of their spiritual ignorance, surrendered to the claims of the Lord Jesus and turned from idols to serve the living and true God.

Is not light cast also on the freeness and the sufficiency of God's mercy? Those souls had been steeped in pagan darkness and enslaved by every conceivable vice, but God, in His loving kindness did not pass them by. Nor can anything other than this mercy cover the sins of those whose conduct may appear to themselves blameless, and who tend to rest in their own righteousness. All have sinned and have come short of the glory of God, but, the grace of God that brings salvation has appeared unto all men.

No power other than that of the Gospel can change the human heart and enable sinners to render obedience, not only to the commands of the law, but to the invitations of the Gospel, and to rest upon Christ as the Rock of their salvation.

But, we ask, how could Barnabas *see* this grace? He saw the effects and the fruits of it in lives changed from being careless and unbelieving to being followers of the Lord. They accepted without question the testimony of Scripture concerning themselves as lost and ruined, and the testimony of Scripture concerning Christ, for the grace that saves works through faith, and such saving faith will prove its reality by its works.

It is not surprising that Paul says to the Ephesian believers that their salvation was to be to the glory of God's grace, and His is the grace of which the fruits were seen in the transformed lives of the converts in Antioch. By their fruits they shall be known.

(2) His reaction to what he saw

Barnabas was glad. Nothing moves the heart of the believer more than the coming of Christ's kingdom in the world, and that for various reasons.

The principal cause of such rejoicing is, we suggest, that God reveals a peculiar measure of His glory in the conversion of sinners. It may be said that the twin strands of God's redemptive purpose in Christ, are the glory of His own name and the salvation of His people. We are familiar with the thought that the chief purpose for man is to glorify God but we must never forget that that was, and is, *God's* chief purpose and aim in the salvation of the Church. In that redemptive purpose of God the glory of His name and the good of His people can never be separated, as is so evident from the High-priestly prayer of the Saviour recorded in the Gospel, where the Son speaks of glorifying the Father and giving eternal life to His people. This thought was before the Psalmist's mind when he declared: "When the Lord shall build up Zion He shall appear in His glory" (Ps. 102:16). In that glory He appears wherever the Holy Spirit is applying the Gospel savingly to needy sinners, but none have eyes to behold the glory save those who are themselves the subjects of God's grace. As more than one colour can be seen whenever the rainbow is visible, so the attributes of the Godhead shine forth in holy splendour when the saving power of the truth is in operation in the hearts of men.

The gladness occasioned by the quickening work of the Spirit arises also from the knowledge that a blessing of inestimable value has been bestowed on poor unworthy sinners. When one thinks of what they had been in their unregenerate days—without hope, and without God in the world—one cannot but feel intensely grateful to God that He has set their faces heavenwards, and their feet in the paths of righteousness. Not for them the condemnation of the law and the terrible doom that awaits all who die Christless. They have peace with God, based on a right and righteous relationship, for their sins are remitted, and they are the sons of God by faith in Christ Jesus. Would not one rejoice in the accession to a fortune of one who had been poor and needy; or in the restoration to health of one who had suffered from a deadly disease? But what is the misery of temporal poverty or bodily illness in comparison with the effects of sin! Therefore no blessing of wealth or health can compare with the riches of God's grace in its ability to bestow happiness upon a human soul. Each believer is an heir of God and a joint heir with Christ.

Another factor that contributed to the gladness felt by Barnabas was, in all likelihood, that his own soul was refreshed by what he saw and heard. Those who have experienced something of the power of the Spirit-charged atmosphere of a rivival can understand, while they cannot describe, the blessedness of feeling in their own hearts, and of sharing with others, the abundant joy of the Holy Ghost. No doubt Barnabas had been praying for the coming of Christ's kingdom, and perhaps had thought of that in terms of the spread of the Gospel throughout Palestine, and the Lord answered in a way that was far above what he had asked or even thought. This is always the manner of God's working, and however much the believer sees of the power of the Gospel, each fresh token of the working of His grace causes, and calls forth, fresh admiration and a holy gratitude that move His people to give the glory to Him alone.

(3) His exhortation to those who had believed

In our consideration of his exhortation to them it is worth noticing how our text sets forth the sovereignty of God and man's responsibility. Their salvation was all of grace, but that salvation was not to be worked out in such a way that exhortation and edification could be dispensed with. In all ages there have been those thoughtless enough to imagine that the doctrine of the sovereignty of God undermined or rendered invalid the doctrine of man's responsibility, but the very opposite is the truth. It is because God is sovereign that we are duty bound to act as responsible creatures, and therefore accountable to Him. It is because we are indebted to grace alone that we ought to render willing and whole-hearted obedience, as those redeemed by the blood of Christ.

Moreover, as we notice, there were to be no exceptions to this rule. He exhorted them all. The Gospel places all believers on the same level as far as relationship to God and relationship to His word are concerned.

Probably all the duties of our Christian religion are comprehended under the one duty that Barnabas urged upon his hearers in Antioch—to cleave unto the Lord, and the word suggests that believers are to make God Himself their goal. Close attention to this counsel would have saved the Lord's people from many a sad situation, and prevented many a tragic happening in the history of the Church. All too often allegiance has been given to a party; liberty of conscience sacrificed to the dictates of a so-called leader, or truth compromised in order not to give offence, all with baneful results for the cause of Truth. Barnabas mentioned neither party nor leader, but directed them to follow Him who alone is worthy of their worship. This did not mean a going forward in the dark, but an advancing in the way of holiness, in accordance with the mind of the Spirit revealed in the Scriptures.

This cleaving to the Lord, moreover, implied the bringing into full exercise of all the faculties of the soul. It is an activity of the head as well as of the heart. It calls, on the one hand, for a holy diligence in the use of all appointed means, and on the other, for a humble dependence upon the grace of God, without which no progress in sanctification can be made.

Those who value most highly the grace that saves, will, of all people, be most conscious of their obligation to follow the Lord in sincerity of heart. Saving faith has Christ, and Christ alone, for its object, but it as surely has the inspired Word for its rule by which the conduct must be regulated, as the believer goes forward to the fulfilment of that destiny for which he has been called by the Spirit.

It would be well for us all to seek this grace. This is the substance of the counsel addressed by the writer to the Hebrews to those who had received a kingdom which could not be moved—let us have grace, and if we receive it we shall inevitably be partakers of the glory.

Let us therefore cleave unto Him until, in God's appointed time He shall, in the words of Zechariah, "bring forth the headstone thereof with shoutings, crying Grace, grace unto it" (Zech. 4:7).

D. GILLIES

THE THORN IN THE FLESH

"And lest I should be exalted above measure through the abundance of the revelations, there was given to me a thorn in the flesh, the messenger of Satan to buffet me, lest I should be exalted above measure."

2 COR. 12:7

It is fascinating to observe how little Paul was esteemed by the Christians of his own day. Despite his many gifts, his unceasing labours and God's evident blessing upon his ministry, he was the butt of constant criticism. The Corinthians were especially vehement in their accusations. He was guilty of levity and vacillation. His motives were according to the flesh. His word was unreliable and self-contradictory, a matter of yea and nay.

In this chapter Paul is coming to a new phase in his answer to these charges: "I will come to visions and revelations of the Lord" (v. 1). God has honoured him, catching him up to the third heaven and granting him such visions and revelations as were unspeakable and which, indeed, it was not lawful for a man to utter. Let us look for a moment at the outstanding features of this experience.

First of all, he was caught up to *the third heaven*. The meaning of this is made plain by the parallel statement in verse four, "he was caught up into paradise". The third heaven is synonymous with paradise, the place of which our Lord spoke to the penitent thief, "Today shalt thou be with me in paradise" (Luke 23:43). It is the place to which the risen Lord has ascended and where those are who sleep in Jesus.

Secondly, Paul cannot be sure whether this experience occurred "in the body or out of the body" (v. 3). It was so vivid that the possibility cannot be dismissed that he was caught up bodily to the third heaven. On the other hand, the experience may have been purely spiritual. He simply cannot tell.

Thirdly, he heard "unspeakable words, which it is not lawful for a man to utter" (v. 4). He heard of aspects of the divine glory which he was personally able to apprehend, but which he was not at liberty to disclose. This is one of many biblical reminders that revelation is not exhaustive. God knows more of His own glory than He has been pleased to reveal; and even Paul, on his own admission here, had seen more than he was permitted to utter.

Finally, something was given to the apostle to counterbalance this privilege: "There was given to me a thorn in the flesh, the messenger of Satan to buffet me, lest I should be exalted above measure." There are some priceless lessons in Paul's teaching at this point. Let us look at it more closely.

(1) The nature of the thorn

What was the nature of this thorn? Many attempts have been made to arrive at a positive and specific identification. Some have suggested malaria, others epilepsy and yet others some form of eye-disease. These enquiries are futile. We must content ourselves with the general features which Paul mentions.

In the first place, it was an experience from which he prayed to be delivered: "I besought the Lord thrice, that it might depart from me" (v. 8). It was not something inseparable from the Christian life, like persecution or temptation or the sufferings of the present time. One could be a Christian without it, as indeed Paul himself had once been.

Secondly, it was satanic. It was "the messenger of Satan to buffet me". It came from the enemy and looked very much like one of the means used by him to hinder or frustrate the Apostle's work. Many a time Paul—and others—must have thought that without it he could have served the Lord ever so much more effectively. Perhaps it made it painful for the Apostle to preach. Perhaps it made it painful for others to listen. We can never know how much anguish lies behind the words, "I was with you in weakness and in fear and in much trembling" (1 Cor. 2:3).

Thirdly, the thorn was *in the flesh*. It was something visible and probably physical and obvious. He speaks to the Galatians of "my temptation which was in my flesh" (Gal. 4:14), and commends them because they did not despise him for it. On his own admission there was a strong temptation for them to do so. There was something about him, off-putting and repulsive, a painful impediment to preaching Christ with boldness.

Yet Paul could *glory* in the thorn. He could be content to have it remain. He could take pleasure in it. He could regard it as God-given. This immediately rules out the possibility that it was something sinful. It is often fatally easy to look at deficiencies in our own characters and say, "That is my thorn in the flesh", and then take comfort from the fact that Paul and other Christians have had these same problems. But this is a perverse wresting of the Apostle's teaching. The thorn is not some sinful propensity or some area of moral and spiritual failure in our own lives. It is not bad temper or lust or irritability or cowardice in Christian witness. Paul could not possibly glory in these or be content that they should remain or regard them as given by God. The thorn is something non-moral and non-spiritual to which no blame attaches. We have absolutely no right to dignify our sins with this title.

Finally, Paul describes this thorn as having a certain function. It was given "lest I should be exalted above measure through the abundance of the revelations". God had given him a unique spiritual privilege, but in the very folds of that privilege there lurked the peril of spiritual pride. He could be exalted and even exalted immoderately. The thorn was given to prevent that. The danger exists for us all, not only for the eminently privileged, but for the recipients of any spiritual blessing and the holders of any spiritual office. It is easy for all of us to imagine that in one sphere at least we out-strip our fellows. It is easy also to forget that we have nothing but what we have received. Hence the counter-poise, the painful, humiliating reminder of our humanness and frailty and dependence, driving us day by day to the conclusion of inferiority and inadequacy.

83

It may be a repulsive physical condition. It may be a disability which seems to hinder our work. It may be deeply painful domestic circumstances. The great thing is that however disagreeable or humiliating it keeps us from being exalted above measure.

(2) Paul's reaction

How, then, did Paul react? "I besought the Lord thrice, that it might depart from me."

We should note that he prayed to "the Lord"—not to God the Father, but to God the Son. Jesus is Lord—Jesus is Jehovah—and therefore we pray to Jesus. Do we take His deity as seriously as that?

Then we see that he prayed with importunity. He besought the Lord *thrice*. He was disturbed by the thorn. He found it difficult to accept. He was desperate that it be removed. How comforting that is! We are so often told, when we find it difficult to be reconciled to God's will, that this is unbelieving and sub-Christian. And yet here is Paul standing in the fellowship of those whose immediate reaction to this kind of experience is that they cannot bear it and that they cannot possibly serve God so long as it lasts and who pray with all earnestness that it go away. It is not that at last Paul is not content. But he has to fight his way through to that. It is neither easy nor instinctive. Often, God's will appears utterly overwhelming, as we see so clearly from the experience of our Lord in Gethsemane. The cup which the Father gave Him filled Him with sore amazement (Mark 14:33) so that, in agony, He prayed with strong crying and tears (Heb. 5:7). Of course, there is an immeasurable gulf between the situation facing Him and any stress to which we may be subject. But His whole bearing underlines the fact that God does not ask that we face adversity with stoical indifference. In many situations, faith can attain composure only through an agony of strong crying and tears.

(3) God's reply

So much for Paul's reaction. But how does the Lord answer his prayer? "My grace is sufficient for thee; for

My strength is made perfect in weakness" (v. 9). Paul's crave is not granted. The thorn is not removed. He must live with it as a permanent accompaniment of his life and labours. That, unmistakably, was God's will for Paul. May it not also be His will for some of ourselves? We have been praying for the removal of certain problems and the elimination of certain painful factors from our lives. Now God is calling upon us to desist. We have no right to persevere with this particular prayer. This pain or embarrassment or hindrance, whatever it may be, is to remain. We have to adjust to it and learn to live with it. In this very context, seemingly so unbearable and impossible, we have to serve and glorify our God.

But from another point of view the prayer is gloriously answered: "My grace is sufficient for thee." Notice Paul's definition of grace. It is not mere pity or mercy or vague intentions of benevolence. It is God's strength put forth redemptively. It is not an emotion, but a power, an enabling and sustaining energy arising out of God's invincible determination to help us.

Note, too, that it is in weakness that this strength is made perfect. Human helplessness is its ideal context. This is where grace is seen in its real glory—in the lives of those who feel hopelessly inadequate in the face of stress and duty and temptation. This is precisely what the thorn did for Paul. It created a profound sense of insufficiency. He might have looked at his gifts and his experiences and his pre-eminent privileges and felt strong and supremely confident. But the thorn prevented that. It made him weak. It filled him with fear. It made him cry, "I cannot possibly serve so long as this thorn remains!" How often has the Lord placed His people in this kind of situation! Calvin had to serve in the face of appalling ill-health. Spurgeon had to preach through constant pain and depression. Whitefield was plagued with a chronic respiratory affliction. How often must these men have cried that if only these problems were removed they could serve the Lord ever so much more effectively! Yet for Paul the thorn was the very condition of his effectiveness, driving him beyond himself to the Christ through whom he could do all things.

(4) Paul's final attitude

This brings us to Paul's final attitude: "Most gladly therefore will I rather glory in my infirmities" (v. 9). But glory in them rather than what? It is not so much that he will glory in infirmities rather than in revelations, but that he will glory in infirmities rather than pray for deliverance from them. He is no longer going to protest to the Lord about them. He is going to glory in them. He is proud of them. Indeed, he takes pleasure in them. He is pleased that they are there. He is glad not simply during them. He is glad because of them.

But how is this possible?

First of all because he sees that they are *given*. They have come from the Lord. They are part of His purpose and He has only one purpose—to present us faultless before the presence of His glory with exceeding joy. The thorn in the flesh makes an essential contribution to that.

Secondly, as we have already seen, these infirmities have a function. Without them he would be exalted above measure. Paul recognises that danger and would rather endure the thorn than fall into the sin of spiritual pride.

Above all, however, he takes pleasure in infirmities, "that the power of Christ may rest on me" (v. 9). That is the most glorious possibility facing him as a Christian. But its fulfilment is conditional. He must be weak—"when I am weak, then am I strong". This was the value of the thorn. It made him weak. It made self-confidence and self-reliance impossible. It placed him in a situation where it was only too vividly clear that he could not face any duty in his own strength. He had resented that. Now he glories in it.

Perhaps through Paul's word here the Lord is calling on ourselves to look again at those factors in our own lives of which we wish to be quit. Is it not possible that but for these, we should be immoderately exalted in self-esteem? Is it not possible that these are the very factors which keep alive the sense of helplessness and incompetence which drives us day by day to Christ? And if so, ought we to resent them? Should we continue to pray for their removal? Ought we not, instead, to glory in them and even, at last, to take pleasure in them?

D. Macleod

SALVATION—THE GIFT OF GOD

"All that the Father giveth me shall come to me; and him that comcth to me I will in no wise cast out." JOHN 6:37

It is one of the remarkàble features of inspired scripture that a portion of truth which confounds and condemns one, comforts and encourages another. Indeed, the same scripture can come to the same person at different times and produce different effects. The Word of God prospers in the thing whereto He sends it, and if at times it acts as a sword "piercing even to the dividing asunder of soul and spirit" (Heb. 4:12), at other times it is a balm which brings relief to the wounded soul and comfort to the broken heart. The Lord's sermon recorded in this chapter was full of hard sayings to hypocrites, but disciples indeed were constrained to exclaim: "Lord, to whom shall we go? Thou hast the words of eternal life" (John 6:68).

Many of those to whom the Lord was speaking refused to acknowledge the claims which He made for Himself, and refused to rest upon Him for salvation. But "what if some did not believe? shall their unbelief make the faith of God without effect?" (Rom. 3:3). Jesus assures His hearers that although they would go in unbelief to a lost eternity He will not lose His people. His sorrow over the Jerusalem that rejected Him was the sorrow of compassion and pity, not the sorrow of frustrated desire and over-turned purpose. All the elect of God shall come to Christ for salvation. He will lose none of His people. He will lose none of His glory. This is a blow to the pride of unbelieving men. It is a truth which has solemn implications for them. "Weep not for me, but weep for yourselves" (Luke 23:28).

But what comfort is in these words for the sinner who is coming to Jesus—no matter at what stage of "coming" he may be! They tell that the grace of God is behind his coming, in his coming, and awaits his coming. This word of grace is a joyful sound to the awakened sinner. The news that God in His grace has provided a complete and effectual salvation is good news indeed to one who has learned by experience the sinful helplessness of man.

We shall endeavour briefly to underline the main aspects of the doctrine of our text, noting

(1) The source of a sinner's salvation

"All that the Father giveth me. . . ."

Here our Lord traces the salvation of a soul—the coming of a soul to Christ for salvation—to the sovereign, electing purpose of God the Father, as it came to gracious expression in the Covenant of Redemption. The river of life flows from *the throne* of God.

The Father is, as Dr. Kennedy of Dingwall put it, the representative of the supremacy of the Godhead, and the fallen human race is in the hands of God as the clay is in the hands of the potter. "Hath not the potter power over the clay, of the same lump to make one vessel unto honour, and another unto dishonour?" (Rom. 9:21). Fallen man had no claim upon God, but God did not lose His claim upon man, and God must press that claim, in whatever way pleases Himself and is in conformity with His own character. He must be glorified in man. Why is God not going to be glorified in the eternal perdition of the whole race? He will be glorified in the eternal condemnation of some, but He is going to be glorified in the eternal salvation of others. Why does God show mercy to any, and why does He show mercy to those to whom He does show mercy? The ultimate reason revealed to us is that it pleased Him to do so. It is for Him to show mercy or not to show mercy just as He wills, until He commits Himself to do so. And having purposed to show mercy it was for Him to choose its objects. No man can claim God's favour on the ground of justice. And no man can claim that because God is merciful He must be merciful to him. "For He saith to Moses, I will have mercy on whom I will have mercy, and I will have compassion on whom I will have compassion" (Rom. 9:15).

"God having, out of His more good pleasure, from all eternity, elected some to everlasting life, did enter into a covenant of grace to deliver them out of the estate of sin and misery, and to bring them into an estate of salvation by a Redeemer" (Shorter Catechism, 20). God's purpose to save, and His choice of those He was to save, was bound up eternally with the purpose to save them through Christ. God never thought of salvation, or of those He was to save, apart from Christ. He was "set up from everlasting, from the beginning, or ever the earth was" (Prov. 8:23). And His people were "chosen in Him before the foundation of the world" (Eph. 1:4). The purpose to save included the provision of Christ as the Saviour.

The entire Godhead is involved in the salvation of a soul. This verse shows the distinction between the Father and the Son, and yet the perfect harmony which exists between them in the work of salvation as in everything else. Christ did not take the work of salvation upon Himself in opposition to the will of the Father. It is not the work of Christ that makes the Father willing to save. The whole work of Christ for His people stems from the fact that the Father devised this way and committed this work into the hands of the Son. God put His people into the hands of Christ that He might be and do all that was necessary for their salvation. As Calvin says, "the donation of the Father is the first step in our delivery into the charge and protection of Christ". "Behold I and the children which God hath given me" (Heb. 2:13).

We tend to think of God's giving of His people to Christ as an act of the past, but here the present continuous tense, "giveth", is used. There is no past, present, or future in eternity, and this decree is eternal. This emphasises the permanence of the decree, or perhaps that the decree is manifest or comes to fruition in the present, in the coming of sinners to Christ. That God gave His people to Christ to save them carries with it the guarantee that they shall come to Him to be saved. "The counsel of the Lord standeth for ever" (Ps. 33:11).

The main point to note is that the sovereign good pleasure of God the Father lies behind the provision of a

Saviour and the coming of sinners to Him. Salvation has its origin in God, in eternity. At its fountainhead salvation is of grace.

(2) The means of a sinner's salvation
". . . shall come to me."

Christ was proclaiming Himself as the bread which came down from heaven—as God's provision for the desperate need of those who are dead in sins. As bread represents what is essential to physical life, Christ is claiming that He is essential to spiritual and eternal life. And as abundance of bread will do no good to one who refuses to eat, so no sinner will receive life from Christ without coming to Him and receiving Him. "Neither is there salvation in any other: for there is none other name under heaven given among men, whereby we must be saved" (Acts 4:12). See that you are not looking to your own works for salvation. But make sure also that you are not presuming upon some general kind of mercy in God, for God's mercy flows to sinners only through Christ.

Christ alone meets the need of the soul because Christ alone meets the requirements of God. Do not think of Christ as just a means of making people happy, and of salvation as merely deliverance from human misery. To be saved is to be saved from sin—to be reconciled to God—to be restored to harmony with God and obedience to His will—to be brought to glorify Him and enjoy Him for ever. To enter into this relationship with God there must be deliverance from the guilt of sin, there must be a positive righteousness in the place of that guilt, and there must be a breach with sin in heart and life. The chief aim of salvation is the glory of God: "that He might make known the riches of His glory on the vessels of mercy, which He had prepared unto glory" (Rom. 9:23). Indeed, salvation is so bound up with the glory of God that the Christian who is looking forward to the consummation of his salvation is said to "rejoice in hope of the glory of God" (Rom. 5:2). It is obvious then that God cannot save in a way that is inconsistent with His glory—that does not reveal the perfection of His character and the harmony of all His attributes. He cannot just overlook sin. Justice as well as mercy must be given full expression if God is to be God. And it is in the Person and Work of Christ that these requirements are met. In the sacrifice of "the Christ, the Son of the living God" (Matt. 16:16), "mercy and truth are met together: righteousness and peace have kissed each other" (Ps. 85:10). In His life and death the law of God has received infinite obedience and satisfaction. Justice as much as mercy must demand that those for whom Christ acted be set free from guilt and accepted by God. And the glory of God is secured in meeting this demand.

Only in Christ can this salvation be secured. As a man He had the necessary relationship to us to be able to act for us, and He had the capacity to suffer and to sympathize. His divinity gave infinite and eternal value and efficacy to all He did as Mediator. And that He is the Christ—the anointed, commissioned Servant of the Father—shows that all His work is in accordance with His will and satisfies His requirements. Thus Christ, alone, is able to save.

But to be saved the sinner must come to Him. Those who are saved by Him are those who are given to Him. That is one side of the matter. The other side is that those who are saved by Him are those who come to Him (John 6:39, 40). "Except ye eat the flesh of the Son of man, and drink His blood, ye have no life in you" (John 6:53). There must be personal appropriation of Christ and of what Christ has done. The sinner must realise that he needs to be saved and that the salvation he needs is in Christ alone. There must be an abandonment of every other scheme of salvation and a willingness to be saved by Christ alone. There must be repentance, forsaking the wicked way, desiring Christ, and resting upon Christ alone for salvation. What is required is not just intellectual acceptance of the truth that Christ saves, but the casting of oneself upon Him for salvation. "He that believeth on me hath everlasting life" (John 6:47).

(3) The sovereignty of grace in a sinner's coming to Christ for salvation

"All that the Father giveth me shall come to me."

There are two sad facts which Christ records of all men in their natural condition: they will not come to Him for life, and they cannot come. Christ is presented in the Gospel in all the glory of salvation as the Saviour who is suitable and free to all. To every lost soul to whom the Gospel comes He cries: "Incline your ear, and come unto me: hear, and your soul shall live" (Isa. 55:3). But without the grace of God sinners have neither the will nor the ability to come to Christ. No matter what pressure is brought to bear upon them by the promises of the Gospel and the threatenings of the law, and no matter how much their emotions may be worked upon, without the grace of God in operation there will be no turning to Christ. The sinner is spiritually dead—not just unable to move towards God or Christ, but an enemy of God. He neither will nor can come because his nature is diametrically opposed to God. Only the almighty, life-giving, renewing grace of God can bring a sinner to Christ.

The grace that gave a people to Christ will bring them to Him, or they would never come. This truth does not limit the Gospel or put a barrier in the sinner's way, as some allege, but gives effect to the Gospel and ensures its success. Of all men without grace it will ever be true that they will not and cannot come, and theirs is the guilt. But grace will bring all whom the Father gives to Christ. They were as dead as others. Some came from strange places and through strange experiences. The devil opposes their coming with all his power. Their sins which should make them run all the faster to Christ keep them back. They feel condemned and excluded. They may have many setbacks. But come to Christ every one of the elect shall, and the sovereign irresistible grace of God is the only explanation.

Coming to Christ is the evidence of election. There is much variety in the details of Christian experience and in the feelings of Christians, but it is true of them all that always they come to Jesus—even when they have to say "Saw ye

Him whom my soul loveth?" (S. of S. 3:3). If you have come to Christ it is because the Father gave you to Christ in an everlasting convenant, and by His Spirit persuaded and enabled you to embrace Jesus Christ, freely offered in the Gospel. The honour of your salvation is His alone. And you know and are glad it is so.

And let those who are still away from Christ remember that it takes the sovereign grace of God to bring a soul to Christ. That is not putting any question mark against the ways of God, but against the condition of your own soul. Man is so depraved, so hostile to God, so unable to do any spiritual good, that although confronted with the awful reality of an eternal hell, and although presented with Christ in all the glory and freeness of the Gospel, he will not flee to the Saviour but when drawn by grace. If you are going to be saved it is only as a debtor to grace for every part of your salvation.

"Rabbi" Duncan put it in a nutshell when he said: "The propositions that grace is necessary, and that it is sovereign, sum up my belief regarding it."

(4) The certainty of salvation for every sinner who comes to Christ

"And him that cometh to Me I will in no wise cast out."

The harmony of the Godhead in salvation is the guarantee that every poor soul who comes to Christ will be welcome. When He says emphatically that He will in no wise cast him out He is showing the certainty of the believing sinner's acceptance, and how different this is from what he deserves. He mentions what the sinner deserves, only to put a double negative on it for all those who come to Him.

To be "cast out" is what every sinner deserves—cast out from all blessing and hope—cast into hell—by the Lamb in the midst of the throne. And that is the destiny of every Christless soul. "And these shall go away into everlasting punishment" (Matt. 25:46).

But on no account will those be cast out who come in faith and penitence, as sinners to Christ. "This man receiveth sinners" (Luke 15:2), no matter how great sinners they have been. Look at the welcome the returning prodigal received. No tongue can express the wonder of the provision that God has made for those who come to Christ. But we know enough when we know that Christ will take them in, for they are complete in Him. To be received by Christ is to "be saved in the Lord with an everlasting salvation" (Isa. 45:17). And this is the encouragement for sinners to come to Christ which the Gospel holds out.

There are two promises in this text: the first gives meaning to the second. For those who believe in the total depravity and inability of man, preaching the Gospel would be a most depressing task if they did not rest in the assurance that the purpose of God shall stand, that all that the Father gives to Christ shall assuredly come to Him. Yet let the sinner who hears the Gospel remember that what he has to do with first of all is not the decree of God but the promise of the Gospel. The first part of the text should keep men from presuming that coming to Christ is something within their own power. You must come to Christ, and whether you can come or not makes no difference to your obligation, or to the sincerity and freeness of the call. But the fact that you cannot come to Christ apart from the drawing power of grace confirms your culpable helplessness and lostness. The second part of the text should keep the awakened sinner from despairing on the ground of the decrees. As C. H. Spurgeon says, "never fear that there is anything in the secret purposes of God which can contradict the open promises of God". Here is all the warrant you need for coming—and remember that this is the language of the One Who is exalted "a Prince and a Saviour, for to give repentance to Israel, and forgiveness of sins" (Acts 5:31).

"All that the Father giveth me shall come to me; and him that cometh to Me I will in no wise cast out."

H. CARTWRIGHT

HE WILL BAPTIZE . . .

"I indeed baptize you with water, but He shall baptize you with the Holy Spirit."
MARK 1:8

One result of today's technological revolution is to make man's activity increasingly mechanised. Much of what before was done by sheer physical effort is now carried out by mechanised and automatic equipment. Many of the calculations and correlations formerly done by the human brain are now taken over by the computer.

Few will dispute that the technological revolution has increased enormously man's capacity to work and so to fulfil God's creation mandate to subdue the earth (Gen. 1:28). On the other hand it has also brought very serious problems one of which is the temptation to view the whole of life in mechanical terms. All too easily we find ourselves thinking that every aspect of our existence can be diagnosed, predicted and organized.

Of course, insofar as our bodies are organized on the basis of motor function, human living has indeed a mechanical aspect. But, according to the Christian Gospel, there is infinitely more to human existence than the operating of a highly complex machine of flesh, bones and brain tissue. The essence of our manhood arises not only from our being created from the dust, but above all from being made in the image of God who is spirit. For this reason the centre of human personality is the spirit or soul, and the most basic elements in our experience—such as love and hate, good and evil—are essentially spiritual realities which cannot be mechanically manipulated, mathematically measured, or scientifically analysed, except in a most superficial way. Motives such as ambition or revenge cannot be fed into a computer. There is this intangible, spontaneous and often unpredictable element in our make-up which defies any precise analysis or control.

It is this element which we tend to lose sight of today. Our obsession with the material and the mechanical at the expense of the spiritual and the spontaneous is seen in the popular attitude to the sacraments. What counts with so many is the mechanics of the operation—the water, the formula, the ritual. If they receive these they are content.

Therefore we do well to heed John the Baptist's reminder here that there are two aspects to this sacrament—the physical and the spiritual, water baptism and Spirit baptism. The clear implication of his words is that the second is far more important than the first. The Church can, and does, baptize with water, but only Christ can baptize with the Holy Spirit. A grasp of this distinction is crucial to a biblical understanding of this sacrament.

These memorable words of John define for us the power of this sacrament, and thus lead us into a deeper understanding also of the privilege of parents presenting their child for baptism and of the position before God of baptized people. We shall notice how our text illuminates all of these three aspects of the sacrament of baptism.

(1) The power of the sacrament ?

John indicates that while he baptizes with water, only Christ baptizes with the Holy Spirit. He is warning his disciples that baptism by him, while highly significant, is not enough. It is preliminary to the great reality which it symbolises—baptism with the Holy Spirit by Jesus.

Similarly the efficacy of Christian baptism does not derive from the Church, the trinitarian formula, or the water, but from Christ and Christ *alone*. And so the Church must say to its people: "We baptize you only with water; Christ alone can baptize you with the Holy Spirit."

At this stage we must ask what John meant by the phrase "baptize with the Holy Spirit"? It helps us to answer this question if we remember that John probably spoke Aramaic, a language closely related to the Hebrew of the Old Testament where the word *spirit*, used to describe the Third Person of the Trinity, basically means "breath" and "wind". It implies both life and power.

The precise meaning of the verb *to baptize* is disputed, but there is little doubt that it was widely used in John's time in connection with *initiation* into a new religion, or the *beginning* of a new religious experience.

Therefore, to be baptized with the Holy Spirit is to begin life in the Spirit, or to be born again of the Spirit. In this experience the Holy Spirit imparts both life and power to our souls which, as a result of sin, are spiritually dead or cut off from God. The close association of water and washing with spiritual regeneration by our Lord (John 3:5) and by Paul (Titus 3:5) may well be allusions to Christian baptism—to the external rite (washing with water) and to the inner reality symbolised (regeneration or new birth).

All this leads us to conclude that it is not water baptism but Spirit baptism which communicates the saving power of God. The notion of baptismal regeneration—that one receives eternal life automatically through water baptism—is alien to the teaching of the New Testament. Water baptism is but the outer form. True, it is a means of grace, but not in the sense that it confers the grace symbolised in it. Rather water baptism is a means of grace in that it points us to the One who alone can confer that grace, to the Lord Jesus Christ. Therefore, unless Spirit baptism precedes, accompanies or follows our water baptism we have the form but not the power of religion (2 Tim. 3:5).

(2) The privilege of the sponsors

Infant baptism is given to parents as the sponsors of their child. A sponsor is a person who acts on behalf of someone else. Parents act as sponsors of their children in a variety of ways. For example, in legal matters a child is represented by one or both parents because he is judged by the law either to be incapable (if an infant) or immature (if a minor). This fact of life operates in the religious sphere also. Because infants are incapable of faith in the Lord Jesus Christ their parents are asked to believe for them, and later, to teach them to believe for themselves.

The practice of *infant* (as distinct from adult) baptism is based upon both a biblical principle and a biblical promise. The principle is that the faith of believing parents brings

97

tneir children into a privileged relationship with God; the promise, that if parents believe, their children will in turn believe.

These—the principle and the promise—are present in every covenant relationship God has entered into with men. For example, to Noah God promised: "And I, behold, I establish my covenant with you, and with your seed after you" (Gen. 9:9). A similar promise is given to Abraham (Gen. 17:7, 8) concerning his descendants of whom God promises "I will be their God". And so we could go on and examine all the recorded covenants made by God with His people—with Jacob (Gen. 35:12), Moses (Deut. 29:10-12), and David (2 Chron. 21:7); in all these cases this promise is central. Therefore it comes as no surprise on turning to the New Testament or Covenant, of which Christ is the mediator, to discover that both the promise and the principle are re-affirmed in the new dispensation. "The promise," says Peter, "is to you and to your children" (Acts 2:39). And the principle is illustrated in Paul's words to the Corinthian Christians: "Your children are holy" (1 Cor. 7:14) where *holy* is used in its primary sense of belonging to God.

The privilege of Christian parenthood rests upon the possession of this promise and the operation of this principle. It is these which enable Christian parents by faith to claim for their children the reality symbolised in this sacrament—engrafting into Christ.

The term *sacrament*, originally a Latin word meaning an (oath or a pledge,) was chosen by the theologians of the early Church to describe the two ceremonies instituted by Christ as a pledge of God's covenant promises to His people. Baptism is like the guarantee we receive with a product stating that the manufacturer will honour his promise concerning its reliability. Now one of the promises pledged through baptism is that the children of believers will be saved.

However, we must not forget that, like many guarantees, this one is not unconditional. Christian baptism is given on the basis of vows which are to be kept in order that the promise be fulfilled. Baptismal vows can be summarised by

98

the words faith and obedience.

First of all, faith. Parents who present their children for baptism have a duty to believe because the promise on the basis of which the sacrament is given is made concerning the children of *believers*. Further, believers must believe, not only on their own account, but also for and about their children. They must actively believe that God will keep this promise, claiming it day by day.

Second, there is obedience. The vows of baptism not only include the faith that our children will be saved, but also our promise to work towards this end by bringing them up in the nurture and discipline of the Lord, teaching and showing them the Gospel of our Lord and Saviour Jesus Christ.

Those of us who are parents of baptized children need to ask ourselves regularly whether in fact we *are* actively and earnestly seeking to fulfil our vows. Are we appropriating this precious promise? Are we seeking to make our children disciples by teaching and showing them the way of Christ? Or do we forget just how great is our privilege and how solemn are our vows?

(3) The position of the spectators

The people involved in a baptismal service are not only the parents and children receiving the sacrament, but also all baptized persons present. Every Christian baptism we witness is a call to renew our baptismal vows. This is the duty not only of Christian parents among the spectators, but also of all baptized people, for the vows taken in the past on our behalf by our parents have, as we have come to the age of responsibility, devolved on us. Therefore, we must ratify or confirm these vows for ourselves. We are no longer young and dependent. Faith is now *our* responsibility.

Yet, is it not the case that, if we were honest, many of us would have to admit that we hang on to the "form" of water baptism much as others do to a lucky charm or mascot? We think that if we have been baptized and have not obviously repudiated our vows this is something that God will give us credit for at the end of the day.

The fallacy of this attitude is seen when we note what

Paul says about a similar dependence by the Jews on the corresponding rite of circumcision. "For he is not a Jew who is one outwardly; neither is that circumcision which is outward in the flesh. But he is a Jew who is one inwardly; and circumcision is that of the heart, in the spirit and not in the letter" (Rom. 2:28, 29). Because of both the general correspondence between the Jewish nation and the Church and the particular correspondence between circumcision and baptism, we may legitimately paraphrase these words in Christian terms as follows: "He is not a real Christian who is one outwardly, nor is true baptism something external and physical. He is a Christian who is one inwardly, and real baptism is a matter of the heart, spiritual not literal."

Or again, we can learn from Paul's insistence that circumcision is of value only if the law is kept. "For circumcision verily profiteth, if thou keep the law; but if thou be a breaker of the law, thy circumcision is made uncircumcision" (Rom. 2:25). By analogy, unless we affirm for ourselves the vows of baptism and keep them, then our baptism becomes un-baptism. I wonder has it ever struck us just how tragically possible it is for us to unbaptize ourselves?

There is this very real danger that water baptism, given to be a blessing, may become a curse if we persist in distorting its functions by trusting in it rather than in Christ. Like all religious forms it is meant to lead us to Christ (Gal. 3:24), but when it, or any other worship form, becomes an end rather than a means, then rather than lead us to Him it cuts off from Him (Gal. 5:4).

What is our position at this moment regarding our baptism? Have we fallen for the fallacy of trusting in the form? Or do we realize that it is only if we trust Christ as our Saviour that the promise of baptism will be fulfilled in our lives? *"answer of a good conscience"*

Conclusion

In conclusion let us never forget that water baptism is only a sign, pointing to the reality of Spirit baptism and therefore substantially different from it. A road sign marked "London 500 miles" is not the city of London. In fact it is a long way from it. Similarly water baptism administered by the Church, while pointing unmistakably to Spirit baptism is something quite different. Let us not rest content with the sign! Let us press on to the reality! Having been baptized with water let us ask Christ to baptize us with the Holy Spirit!

F. A. J. MACDONALD

CHRISTIAN DISCIPLESHIP

"I will follow thee . . ."

MATT. 8:19

"I will follow Him." Do you remember when you first made that promise—or was it a vow? You believed you were utterly sincere. Nothing was too much for Jesus. In the light of the Cross, in the light of forgiveness; in the experience of forgiveness; in the joy of gospel peace; in the fulness of your personal surrender, you made the vow and truly meant it. Yet the truth is you did not fully know what was involved. How much you had to learn in the school of Christ! Have you been disappointed in Him as well as in yourself? Is it possible that you have become a bit "worldly wise" while teaching the mechanics of Salvation? Have you become a little cynical? Has the foolishness of preaching become to you foolishness? We perhaps long for New Testament Power, but we often forget how Power expresses itself. We want to be a powerful minister or home missionary or ordinary Christian witness and to feel the thrill of being useful and breaking through. We often want the power of Christ more than the Cross of Christ, or the power without the Cross. Perhaps we feel we've heard all this before, in fact preached it! If we put into words the thoughts that brood in the heart they may say—"It doesn't work". In a sense we are right. "It doesn't work." Power without a Cross never works. The Bible has much to say concerning Power. Remember Paul . . . "That we may know Him and the power of His Resurrection". Yes, Him first, and the Resurrection Power second.

Never reverse the order!

Perhaps we might do well to go back to Matthew's school to find afresh the portrait of a saint. Let us try to see the portrait in the frame of Matthew 8:9. . . .

This confession is so often made and yet its implications are so seldom realized. Follow where? . . . to obscurity? . . . to deprivation? . . . to outside the crowd? The Son of Man has still nowhere to lay His head. To develop as a disciple we must first, of necessity, recognize who He is. Is He a Royal King, possessor of Eternal Power or just someone who gets us out of a jam? If the first He cannot change. He is the same now as then. Matt. 9:9, 27 gives a true picture. Remember the Centurion? "I am a man under authority, having soldiers under me: and I say to this man, 'Go', and he goeth; and to another, 'Come', and he cometh; and to my servant, 'Do this', and he doeth it. . . . Speak the word only and my servant shall be healed." Yes, a Royal King. In 8:27 "What manner of man is this that even the winds obey Him". A supernatural, timeless King. . . . God's Blessed Son. We must never lose sight of the Saviour. It was He who shed Blood! He who agonized! He who atoned! He who promised! He who commands!

"I will follow Him. . . ." What does this entail?

(1) God's first demand

The portrait begins to take form—the form of a true servant for all time. Minister, missionary, elder or young Christian. Matt. 5:44 is God's first demand. "Love your enemies." What has this to do with power? What has this to do with sanctification? Just this . . . He demands that we accept His standards whatever they be. Love your enemies; Be ye holy as I am holy; the fruits of the Spirit as in Galatians, i.e. meekness, lowliness, love, joy, peaceableness. There are no short cuts, no lesser demands for some. If we accept less we call Him to cut off our power. His standards get progressively higher. When He says, "Love your enemies" He is not only asking us to do one particular thing but is laying down a standard for everything. His standard . . . nothing less!

(2) Wholehearted service

Wholehearted service comes next. Matt. 6:24, "No man

can serve two masters for either he will love the one and hate the other or else he will hold to the one and despise the other. You cannot serve God and mammon!" Not a foot in each camp. We may be tempted, yes we will be tempted. Yet Christ demands wholehearted service. Not only is serving two masters difficult, it is impossible, it just can't be done! If we are holding back anything—sinful or legitimate—at that moment we are serving Satan and self. The acceptance of persecution as a common lot is promised in Matt. 10:16–20 and this is often hard to stomach, especially social persecution. To be socially ostracised is not easy on flesh and blood. Jesus says, "Beware of man"— the subtle dig—the scornful sneer—the scowling scoff— yes and worse. This is something the flesh always hates and fears, something we shun, yet something which is promised. "I will follow you" is sometimes so difficult when it leads to the school of persecution. Open witness is a full prime requirement and the call is accepted with a fearful threat. "Whosoever shall confess Me before men, will I confess before My Father. Whosoever shall deny . . . him will I deny . . ." (Matt. 10:32). Before men—yes men of all sorts . . . open sinners, scoffers, intellectual superiors, social leaders! Courage comes before triumph! Honesty comes before success! This is what we are all called to. There is no road of escape and we ought not to want one.

In Matt. 10:37 utter allegiance is called for. "He that loveth father or mother more than Me is not worthy of Me." The knife goes deep. The soul will bleed. Note that "more than Me". The demand to utter allegiance is great, yet it does not destroy family love, but places it in its true perspective. Yet how hard! Do we complain at this point? Do we murmur? This is not worthy of Me. Is there a situation just now which is challenging this allegiance? Are you facing conflict? Is the battle fierce? Remember then "more than Me". "I will follow Thee." Does it not grow progressively harder?

Matt. 11:6 demands an acceptance of all His providences. "Blessed is he who is not offended in Me." John in the darkness of doubt cried out, "Art Thou He that should come or do we look for another?" The cry from this dark

dungeon is always the same, "Have I made a mistake?"
Ought I to have begun this Christian work? Ought I to
have started training for the ministry? Ought I to have
come to the mission field? The subtlety of the serpent is
seen here. Why did this or that happen? I expected things
to be different. Brethren, it is the Leader who makes the
policy, we just follow. Why, thought John, does not Jesus
intervene here? I have prayed, cried, longed, thought and
tried. Jesus wants us to surrender to His Providence. You
are fitting in to His Plan. You are acknowledging His
Purpose when you don't understand. Not, have I made a
mistake about my conversion, and need it renewed? Not,
have I made a mistake about my call, and need it renewed? Not, have I been deceived by myself—for the
Gospel is preached and is successful.

> Not till the loom is silent,
> And the shuttles cease to fly,
> Will God unroll the canvas,
> And reveal the reason, why,
> The dark threads are as needful
> In the weaver's skilful Hand,
> As the threads of gold and silver,
> In the pattern He has planned.

To say I will follow in the darkness is to advance in the
school of Christ. An acknowledgment of all His brethren
as ours, is a mark of true discipleship.

Matt. 12:45–50 says: "Whosoever doeth the will of my
Father the same is my mother and brother and sister."
This concept demands developing grace and wisdom.
John 3 is "Whosoever will. . . ." Matt. 12 is "Whosoever
does. . . ." Our brother may make mistakes, and have all
the sins of immaturity, carnality, inefficiency, smugness or
even worse. The question we must ask is really this. "Is he
trying to do the will of God? Is he trying . . . even so weakly?"
Then they are your brethren. You must love, care, pray,
help them as Christ helps you. You must give them the
place and position He gives them. You need not agree with
them on everything, but you must agree with everything
Christ says about them and everything Christ would do
for them.

(3) The conditions for continuing discipleship

Matt. 16:24 gives the conditions for continuing discipleship. "If any man will come after me, let him deny himself, take up the Cross, and follow me." Self-denial, self-destruction, self-abasement.

There is no such thing as self-denial and going our own way. Self-destruction involves the Cross. Self-abasement involves following Him. His Way . . . His Paths . . . not ours! These are ever the present demands of discipleship. They do not change when the going is tough. They do not change on the Home Field or on the Mission Field. They do not change because of failure—either personal or united. The human will must ever be crushed; self-trust must always feel the touch of the Cross; human wisdom must always bow where Jesus leads. In order to follow we need daily what Matt. 17:9 shows clearly. The supreme vision of Jesus only. "They saw none save Jesus only." To begin with they saw the Law and the Prophets—then—Jesus only! Supreme in the estimation of His Father, He must become supreme in their estimation. When He is seen supreme in the estimation of His Church, whatever our problems (trial difficulty, etc.) the only true and satisfying answer is seen in the light of "Jesus only". Love for Jesus only; the vision of Jesus only; work for Jesus only, hardship for Jesus only; labour for Jesus only. If we have the vision we have the strength. If we lose the vision we lose the strength!

Matt. 18 continues, and the portrait takes deeper form. He demands the pattern of childlikeness. "Whosoever shall humble himself as this little child the same shall be greatest in the Kingdom of Heaven." The principles on earth are as in heaven—the example of the little child coming quickly, obeying immediately and trusting implicitly . . . is ever an illustration for each generation. His undoubting assurance, willing obedience and unclouded trust seem to be the daily demand here. Is it so with us? Are we childlike or childish? Is our trust in Jesus today clouded by doubt, defeat, disillusionment or denial? Is our obedience at this moment joyous, willing and confident? Is ours an undoubting assurance in spite of the difficulties we find even when we find them insoluble? . . . in spite of the mountainous task? . . . Are we childlike in our Christian service or are we in the group who "know better"?

Matt. 18 demands, integrity in personal dealings. "If your brother shall trespass against you go and tell him" . . . not others . . . tell God and him. How much trouble would be avoided, how much pain eased, how much trust continue, how many difficulties overcome if this command were obeyed instead of worldly wisdom practised? Some may fear to speak. If you fear to say anything to a brother, fear to talk about him to another!

Matt. 18:22. The portrait continues to take form in Christ's call to be forgiving. Forgiveness is a state of mind as well as a series of acts. Seventy times seven is the demand and who among us has not asked God for forgiveness this same number of times? In case some do not see the spirituality of this command let us add . . . "Forgive your enemies . . . those who despitefully use you". Know the joy of being a forgiver. It is Christ's standard.

Matt. 19:21, 29. Discipleship becomes even more demanding. The rich young ruler comes in to the picture now. Through him we are called to relinquish all. A glance at verse 21 is frightening. . . . It is not only riches and ambition but mother, father, wife and children! We began by relinquishing all. We must continue under the same principle. How hard at the outset! How much harder during the course!

We must go farther in Matt. 20:26. We are not only to accept all believers but be servants to all! "Whosoever shall be great let him be your minister." A life spent in ministry, serving, helping and emptying is a life well spent. The Master's experience is that of washing feet! Love is needed—patience is needed—strength of character is needed—simplicity is needed. We must wash the feet of the doubter. He did! Wash the feet of the denier. He did! Wash the feet of the forsaker. He did! Even the betrayer. He did! This is the way to power. Out of love today we must wash the feet of the self-important and the weak, by putting ourselves out. We must pour ourselves out for all.

In Matt. 22:9 we find the servant's call to service. This

is a call to every Christian in every generation. We find it in the parable of the field—in the words *"go" "find" "bid"*. *Go* from the plans of self-interest, perhaps from the comfort and even the smugness of evangelical fellowship. Go from the activities which are legitimate, from the comforts you enjoy. Go from the friends who would hold you back. Go when surrounded by weariness and fatigue. Go, find: . . . where are they? In the pagan tribes, the materialistic homes, in their Godless occupation, in their hell inspired pleasures. . . . Go and find! Remember what C. T. Studd said, "Some want to live within the sound of church and chapel bell. I want to start a workshop within a yard of hell!"

Bid them! Go! Find! Bid! Bid them. Plead with them; woo them; help them; pull them; pray them, with a Godly life and a loving Gospel . . . yes even with a frightened heart. This is following Him.

(4) The demand for continual self-abasement

Matt. 23 leads us farther in the next demand . . . the demand for continual self-abasement. "Whosoever shall exalt himself shall be abased, and he that humbleth himself shall be exalted."

No matter how far we have developed in the school of Christ this command is never withdrawn. It comes to the minister as to the junior missionary . . . to the Superintendent as to the recruit. Just how many human problems would never have had to be faced if this command for true discipleship had been kept! That jealous seed would never have blossomed and that resentment would have had no roots. There is no room for love of place in the school of Christ. It does not say where we should humble ourselves, but rarely are we found looking for the opportunity. We look for other opportunities, other recognitions, but to humble ourselves . . . ah, that's different. Unrest, bitterness, antagonism and suspicion are all the children of personal exaltation. They should have been slaughtered at birth and would have been had we obeyed this command of the Lord.

So the way is hard. Perhaps your strength has ebbed, your

faith is flickering, your call is just a faint echo . . . but now is the time for Matthew's brush in 24 and 13. We need to keep on enduring. "He that endureth to the end shall be saved." Yes, he that *keeps on* enduring is the sense of the word. It is true that we must endure through something . . . be it temptation, personal weakness, fear, coldness, lack of vision, little results, bleak prospects . . . but to endure is not just putting up with it. It is more than that. It is active not passive. It is to face the problems knowing what they entail, whether personal or otherwise, even when they seem insoluble. With one hand on the impossible stretch the other out and touch the God of the impossible. It is the stretching out that is enduring.

Matt. 24:42 gives wise counsel for all time. "Be watchful. Watch therefore for ye know not what time your Lord doth come."

These words can be written over many things. We know not the power of Satan or his subtlety despite our years in the battlefield. We know not the deceitfulness of our own hearts or the indwelling sin. We know not our pride and love of position. We know not our base desire always to be thought right. "Be watchful" says Matthew, as a sentinel in a castle . . . as a mother looks out for the good of her young ones . . . as the guard at the front line. Don't underestimate your enemy. Don't over estimate yourself!

(5) Christian humanity

The portrait of the saint is nearing completion. Matthew just added the finishing touches in 25 and 40. "In as much ye did it unto one of the least of these my little ones, ye have done it unto Me." Matthew here pleads for Christian humanity. He makes the tremendous statement that an action done to any out of love to Christ is accepted as an act done personally for Him. Is Christian humanity anything less than Christ-likeness? See Him minister to the hungry crowd. So must we! See Him visit the homes of the outcasts . . . so must we! There was no one so bad as to be outside the scope of Christ's Blood and so none must be outside ours. He measures the wearisome chores out of love to Him.

When we are tired it is like virtue going out for Him. He measures persistence in the face of all the things which annoy, as love to Him. His yardstick is not ours. It is not just listening to the Word, but He is looking for the Word in action. It is not just the attitude of prayer but prayer in action. It is not only pressing food for the soul but often providing food for the body. To have Christ-likeness we must be good, kind, helpful. This is truly being evangelical.

Such is the stuff disciples are made of! When Matthew sees the woman breaking the box of alabaster ointment on Jesus' head (ch. 26 and 7), *he is still finishing off the portrait by putting the value on Christ.* How do you really value Him? What is He worth? The ointment surely symbolized an out-poured life. Certainly it is precious . . . very precious . . . but is He worth it? "Greater love hath no man than this, that a man lay down His life for His friends." Is this the value you put on Christ? Your life with all its possessions, talents, gifts, opportunities. Is your life a daily sacrifice? Is it a daily consecration? When you said, "I will follow Thee," did you mean an outpoured, sacrificed, consecrated life daily? Do you value Christ above your life?

Matthew now finishes the portrait with the Lord's command. In 28 and 19 he reiterates, "Go to the ends of the earth; teach at the ends of the earth; I AM at the ends of the earth." Where He sends He is!

I think then, as I look at Matthew's portrait, that I see the power of God at work in the midst of human experience. This power seems to be expressed in character more than in feelings. What a standard Matthew sets and yet this is what it means to follow Him. . . . We may say, "Who is sufficient for these things?" We will have our part in His strength if we see that not only is doctrinal assent required but develop-ment from the seed of the New Birth. Christianity is not necessarily a feeling of triumph . . . of always being on top of the world. Sometimes it is a fight against the odds, a swimming against the tide, and a fight against such utter personal weakness that we must find Christ afresh daily or face personal tragedy.

Let us think again. "I will follow Him." Will we? . . . even if it means Matthew's way? Let us commit ourselves anew in dependence upon God's grace. "I will follow Him." "Yes I will." "I will accept His standards. I will offer whole-hearted service. I will face persecution. I will start afresh an open witness. I will give utter allegiance. I will accept all His Providences no matter how dark. I will acknowledge His brethren and my brethren. I will by His grace go the way of self denial and self involvement. By His grace I will continue to be watchful. I will practise Christian humility. I will set a value on Christ such as the woman with the alabaster box did.

This then is what is entailed in being a Christian . . . a disciple of Christ. This is what it means to say, "I will follow Him". Of course we can't do it without His strength, but how often we refuse to meet the conditions. We refuse to come to the place where His strength is found. Christ must then break us before we come to that place. Perhaps at the moment we are in the process of being broken, we are feeling His way hard, difficult, strait and sore. Hear again what He says to His disciples. "Those whom I love, I chasten." "Those who bear fruit, I purge . . . that they may bring forth more fruit." Let us never make the mistake of thinking that power is merely a feeling. Power is the life of Christ expressed.

D. PATERSON

GOD'S PEOPLE IN A
HOSTILE WORLD

*"But the God of all grace, who has called us unto His eternal glory
by Christ Jesus, after that ye have suffered a while, make you perfect,
stablish, strengthen, settle you"*   I PET. 5:10

Peter is writing to groups of Christians in Asia Minor, weak
and isolated, with little opportunity of fellowship with other
Christians. Around were hostile pagans, and perhaps still
more hostile Jews. They were suffering persecution, and
they feared worse to come. Peter does not comfort them with
wishful thinking. He can hold out no hope of respite. His
aim is to put iron into their blood. He does not expect them
to escape trial, nor does he particularly wish that they
should. He does desire that in the hour of trial, they should
acquit themselves as Christians ought. The message of our
text is addressed to Christians in a hostile world. The world
is hostile still, and increasingly so. The message remains
apposite today.

(1) **The Christian's situation**

The peculiarity about the Christian is that he lives in two
spheres.

1. He is in Christ. The phrase "by Christ Jesus" can also
be rendered "in Christ Jesus". You remember how Paul
speaks of himself as "a man in Christ". The position of the
Christian as in Christ is indeed fundamental to Paul's
thinking. The Christian is united by faith to Christ in a
relationship as intimate as that of a member of the body to
the head. God looks at Christ, and in Him He sees all
believers. God looks at each believer and sees him in Christ.
Because he is in Christ he is secure as Christ Himself is
secure. Satisfaction for his sins has been made by Christ,

and it has been accepted on his behalf as if he had made the satisfaction himself. Moreover, the knowledge that he is in Christ affects the believer's character. It should colour his every decision. The mind of Paul dwells much on this. The believer when he rejoices, rejoices in the Lord, when he marries, he does so in the Lord, when Christian children are enjoined to obey their parents, they are to do so in the Lord; when the believer makes his plans he does so in the Lord, that is to say, he seeks to make his plans according to the mind of Christ. It is not only that this ought to be the case. The believer, being united to Christ by faith, is a child of God, and that fact must be evident, at least to some extent, in his character. We read that "Everyone that doeth righteousness is born of Him". This means that sin in the believer is out of character. It is there, sad to say, but it is out of character. You know what we mean by that. A father has a son who does something wildly out of keeping with the character he had fondly ascribed to him. We can hear him say in the grief of a broken heart, "That is not like my son". Can we say that God is grieved? Of course we can. Does not Paul say "Grieve not the Holy Spirit of God?" How much grief we must cause to the Holy Spirit of God in a single day—every day! Yet in spite of all our lapses our standing remains.

But if his children shall forsake my laws and go astray,
And in my judgments shall not walk But wander from my way:
If they my laws break and do not keep my commandments;
I'll visit then their faults with rods, their sins with chastisements.
Yet I'll not take my love from him, nor false my promise make.
My covenant I'll not break, nor change what with my mouth I
     spake.

We should remember the faithfulness of God when we are tempted to despair of ourselves. We should remember it too when we are tempted to criticize others. Who are we to judge? If a person is in Christ, God has accepted him.

That then is one side, and, let us remember, the more important side—the Christian is a man, or a woman, in Christ. But

2. The Christian, who is in Christ, is at the same time in the world, and, because of this double sphere in which he

moves, there is tension, and hence there is suffering. There is, of course, suffering which is common to all mankind, and the Christian does not escape. But there are sufferings which are peculiar to the Christian; and even such sufferings as he shares with the world take on a new meaning. They are all part of God's discipline to further his sanctification— "After that ye have suffered . . .".

(a) There is suffering which is of the nature of chastisement. The Christian may have to suffer sickness, pain, loss, disappointment, and sorrow. We are not suggesting that every such experience is to be traced to some particular sin. To try to connect sin and suffering in this way can become a morbid obsession. On the other hand we should seek to accept everything that comes our way as part of God's discipline—perhaps to solemnise us, perhaps to lift our thoughts from things temporal to things eternal, and to shew us the folly of building for this world, but always to further our growth in grace. It is true that some have to endure more suffering than others. Jacob had a life of more severe trial than Abraham or Isaac. We do not know why. Perhaps he was made of more intractable material. In the end of the day he could speak with gratitude of "the God who hath fed me all my life long unto this day; the Angel which redeemed me from all evil". The Christian can rest assured that

"My Father's hand shall never cause His child a needless tear."

The silversmith heats the furnace, not because he hates the silver, but because he wants it as pure as it can be made.

(b) There is also suffering which is of the nature of conflict. We are engaged in a warfare from which there is no discharge. We have enemies without and enemies within. Verse 8 leads us to the root of it all. "Your adversary, the devil, goeth about as a roaring lion, seeking whom he may devour." We speak of the temptations of the world, the flesh, and the devil, but the primary source is the devil. *The devil uses the world.* Those to whom Peter was writing were experiencing this in an acute form. They were subject to persecution, or, at least, to the constant threat of persecution. Today, in this country, persecution is absent in its cruder forms. But the difficulty of living the Christian life in a hostile world is always present. Think of a young Christian witnessing for Christ before hostile or indifferent companions. Think of the howl of protest the world raises when anyone in the name of God tries to thwart its selfish plans. Think of the mockery that often greets a statement of the Christian Gospel, or even an assertion of Christian moral standards. Think especially of the subtle influences that cool our ardour, that mute our witness, that lead us to compromise. *The devil also attacks us through the flesh*, that is to say, through ourselves. We are not ignorant of his devices. We know with what cleverness and subtlety he works. He is busy when we have had a season of blessing, for if he can catch us off our guard, he can rob us of much of the blessing received. He is never more dangerous than when he is quiescent. We are flattering ourselves that we are making progress, and, just then, the devil is planning a more devastating attack. We find ourselves like the allied armies in France during the "phoney war" of 1939–40, being told that Hitler had "missed the bus", and believing it, until he arrived in a cloud of aeroplanes and a swarm of tanks.

We may think of some of Satan's methods.

(*a*) He sows seeds of unbelief. He tries to make us doubt the foundation truths of the Christian faith. He instils doubts as to whether we can really claim the power of God, and thus undermines our Christian lives.

(*b*) He sows discord among brethren. He plants seeds of suspicion, he exploits natural antipathies, and so breaks the fellowship of Christian people.

(*c*) He makes the most of our frailties. He has studied us more deeply than any psychoanalyst. He knows our weak points, he knows when we are weary, or not in good health, or inclined to be careless, and he works upon that knowledge ruthlessly.

Such is the situation. What hope can we have? Peter holds out no prospect of respite. He does direct us to recollect the Christian's assets.

(2) The Christian's assets

What have we to set against so powerful an adversary? Peter mentions two things.

1. *The inspiration of a noble calling.* God has called us to "His eternal glory". Does that mean that we are called to happiness for ever in heaven? No doubt! But that is a poor paraphrase. Glory is far greater than happiness, eternal means far more than lasting for ever, and this is a calling which though fulfilled in heaven, is entered upon now. What then is "His eternal glory"? Is it not just the character of God? Can you imagine a more salutary thought than that we are called on to reflect His character? "When He shall appear, we shall be like Him". That is the ultimate goal— that we should reflect His likeness, and towards the attainment of that goal all God's dealings are directed. Towards that goal our eyes should be set. That we may progress towards that goal our eyes should be fixed upon Jesus. "We all, . . . beholding as in a glass the glory of the Lord, are changed into the same image from glory to glory."

2. We are reminded of *The availability of inexhaustible resources.*

"The God of all grace!" That is the answer to "your adversary the devil". The word "grace" is a great word. It reminds us first of all that we are undeserving. God's gifts have been merited by nothing in us. It reminds us of the price at which these gifts have been made available. "Ye know the grace of our Lord Jesus Christ, that though He was rich, yet for your sakes He became poor that ye through His poverty might be rich." It reminds us also of the munificence of God's gift. The word seems to sum up all that is made available to us in Christ. There is *justifying grace* by which we sinners are accepted as righteous, because the righteousness of Christ—His obedience to God's law, and His satisfaction on the Cross for our disobedience—is accredited to us as if we had done it all. There is *reconciling grace* by which we who were enemies are made friends and not only friends, but sons and daughters of Almighty God. There is *illuminating grace* to guide us through each perplexing path of life. There is *restraining grace* to keep us from turning aside out of the right way. There is *restoring grace*

to heal our backsliding and to return us to the paths of
righteousness. There is *sustaining grace* to uphold us in times
of sorrow, and in those times when everything seems to go
wrong. There is *strengthening grace* to enable us to face
temptation and to prevail.

> Against me earth and hell combine,
> But on my side is power divine.
> Jesus is all, and He is mine.

What excuse then can there be for failure? The word
"cannot" should not be in the Christian's vocabulary. What
God commands, He gives grace to perform.

So, finally, we are bidden to believe,

(3) The Christian's promises

The words of our text can be treated as future tenses,
and so can be taken as promises—"shall perfect, shall
stablish, shall strengthen, shall settle". I want you to look at
these words for a moment. Some of them are very interesting
and must have been precious to Peter.

1. *Shall perfect.* The word means "repair" or "restore".
Tradition has it that Mark received much of the material
for his Gospel from Peter. We can imagine how Peter
would have told him of the day when Jesus called Andrew
and himself from their fishing boats, and then called James
and John when they were mending their nets, and as Mark
sets down the story, the word he uses is this word.

Fishermen must mend their nets; and as Peter looked
back on his experience as a fisher of men, he realised that
not only nets need to be repaired. The fisherman needs to
be repaired too. If the fishing is good, it takes toll of our
energies and spiritual resources. If the fishing is bad, it
leaves us disquieted and depressed. I am sure Peter often
felt himself more desperate than a torn net. But he knew
One who restores, and refits for service.

2. *Shall stablish.* Here again is a word that had a gracious
history for Peter. When Jesus foretold his denial, He added,
"When thou art converted, strengthen (stablish) thy
brethren. This is the word that Jesus used. Peter's denial
was a shameful, bitter, and humbling experience. It
shattered his self-confidence. But it led him to God-

confidence. He was not only restored, he was stablished, so that he became rock-like in his steadfastness. Now he is shewing his brethren how they can be stablished as well.

3. *Shall strengthen.* So shall we be strong for every battle we have to fight.

4. *Shall settle.* The word means to ground upon a sure foundation, like the man whose house was founded upon a rock.

That brings us back to the primary question. Are we building on the right foundation? Can we say

> "My hope is built on nothing less than Jesus' blood and
> righteousness?"

If not, none of the gracious promises to God's people applies to us. But we need not remain in this woeful condition. The Gospel invitation is still open. Nay more, the command rings in our ears, "Seek ye the Lord while He may be found, Call ye upon Him while He is near". There is also the promise, "Let him return unto the Lord, and He will have mercy upon him, and to our God, and He will abundantly pardon". Then, if our lives are resting upon this sure foundation, whatever be our lot, we can claim all the promises of God. They are guaranteed to us in Christ, and we shall be "Kept by the power of God through faith unto salvation".

H. G. MACKAY

SHINING IN THE DARK

"And the Syrians had gone out by companies, and had brought away captive out of the land of Israel a little maid; and she waited on Naaman's wife." 2 KINGS 5:2

If our information on the little Hebrew maid were limited to this verse we would have a touching but pointless little story of how rough soldiers in a border raid had captured a young girl and carried her far away from home and friends to be a slave in a great man's house. It was but one of those domestic tragedies that are inseparable from times of war. Our feelings would be touched as we think of the heartbreak within her and the grief back home where her youthful presence no longer brightened the lives of her loved ones, and we would be moved with pity only, without any compensating thoughts. But as the story unfolds our pity is all but displaced by wonder as we discover how an overruling God employs her to point her afflicted master to the source of healing.

The first lesson we wish to gather from this incident is,

(1) The blessing of a Christian home

No details are furnished of her background or upbringing but there are some things we may lawfully read into the story of the little maid.

In the absence of any reference to the unusual we assume the usual and this is that the Christian home is the normal means in the providence of God of leading us to an acquaintance with Himself. That the Hebrew maid had such an acquaintance with the God of Israel we hope presently to show. Not only do we feel warranted, then, in assuming a good upbringing but we even discover some of the lines that her upbringing followed.

She had evidently been *taught to pray*. Her first utterance betrays this—"Would God!" This is the language of prayer. We have the very same expression, though differently rendered, in the opening verses of the 119th Psalm: "O that . . .!" It is the expression of a heartfelt wish or longing directed Godwards. Such breathings heavenwards commonly receive their first encouragement in the Christian home.

The Hebrew maid had also been taught *respect for her superiors*. This she had obviously learned was the implication of the fifth Commandment and her understanding pointed to some tuition regarding the spirit as well as the letter of the law. Although she was a member of the chosen race and Naaman of alien blood, and though her menial position in his household was one that had been thrust upon her, with all the bitter resentment that that might well have engendered, she yet refers to him with the utmost deference as, "my master".

Again, part of her upbringing consisted in *an acquaintance with sacred things*. She knew of the Lord's prophet, although her king did not (cf. v. 8). Nor was her acquaintance vague and undefined as of one out of touch—she knew the prophet's whereabouts, she was instructed as to the exalted nature of his office and revered him as the servant and representative of the God of Israel for whom nothing is too hard. In this respect particularly, her training had obviously differed most markedly and with the healthiest results from that of the young hooligans of Bethel who mocked that same holy man's personal appearance and beliefs (2 Kings 2:23).

(2) A personal faith

What we are most interested to find is that by the blessing of God, the little maid's early instruction had issued in a personal faith—which is of course the end to which all such instruction is directed. "And thou Solomon my son know thou the God of thy father, and serve Him with a perfect heart and with a willing mind" (1 Chron. 28:9). The maid whom we meet here is obviously living on no second-hand experience—she has something of her very own. Indeed it is doubtful if anything less would survive in her situation. But such first-hand religion is what the promise of God leads us to expect will result from early training. "Train up a child in the way he should go and when he is old he will not depart from it" (Prov. 22:6). How wonderful an experience too when you come to seek God for yourself and discover to your delight that you have found your father's and your mother's God and "not another". And Jacob said, "O God of my father Abraham and God of my father Isaac, the Lord which saidst unto me . . ." (Gen. 32:9).

It is of course necessary to remember that no amount of training and example will of themselves lead us to the Lord: His own blessing, along with these means, is essential. This is illustrated somewhat in this very chapter by the contrast between the Hebrew maid and Gehazi. The prophet's personal attendant could hardly have been in closer touch with the things of God—but all to no effect. Like an Old Testament Judas his heart is set on material things, he is ensnared by wordly ambition, led into deceit and lying to further his proud aims and finally passes off the scene under a curse. The divine blessing is indispensable to give efficacy to the means of grace. The children of the kingdom are "born, not of blood nor of the will of the flesh, nor of the will of man, but of God" (John 1:13).

We are not told at what stage in her young life the vital change came over the little Hebrew maid. It may have been while she was still at home—in which case her loved ones would have less cause for alarm when she was launched so violently into the world. The Lord whom she trusted would watch over her and be the "guide of her youth" (Prov. 2:17). Or did she leave home still in a natural state? And was she impelled in her exile and loneliness to seek her parents' God and discover for herself His reality and nearness? We cannot tell. It is enough that she had found Him and rested there.

We have claimed that the little Hebrew maid had "the root of the matter" in her. We adduce the evidence, first, in the confidence she expresses that her master will be cured if only he can secure contact with the prophet in Israel. Now this was remarkable faith because we are distinctly told that Elisha had wrought no such miracle before.

"Many lepers were in Israel in the time of Eliseus the prophet; and none of them was cleansed saving Naaman the Syrian" (Luke 4:27). To believe where things are decidedly against you is real faith. She had moreover this difficulty to surmount—Elisha was a prophet to Israel and to none besides. How could she persuade herself that the healing power could be stretched and accommodated to heal a Syrian? Had she an inkling of the scope of the Gospel which, while coming to the Jew first, extends to the uttermost parts of the earth? It could well be, for God "hides these things from the wise and prudent and reveals them to babes" (Matt. 11:25). Like someone of her own sex long after—Mary of Bethany—whose vision surpassed that of the very disciples, the little maid may have had an insight into "things to come". Or perhaps she uttered words the full prophetic import of which she herself scarcely gauged.

Most convincing of all in proof of her personal piety was the compassion and spirit of forgiveness that underlay her longing to see her master made whole. The circumstances in which she came to be under his roof at all might well have embittered her so far as to make her look with secret satisfaction on his dreadful disease. In this she might have found some compensation for her enforced exile from her father's home. What a sweet revenge to the natural heart! But she was a stranger to such feelings. If they arose she had conquered them. Though she had never heard of the Lord's prayer she had imbibed its spirit—"forgive us our debts as we forgive our debtors, and lead us not into temptation but deliver us from evil" (Matt. 6:12). Nothing therefore will please her more than that her master might recover from his leprosy.

Add to her faith and her compassion her open testimony to what she believed and felt. Many people since then may have shared her innermost feelings but at such a tender age and in such alien surroundings have been too timorous to express them. Nor was there lacking the distinct possibility, indeed probability, of her testimony being spurned. To speak of what Israel's prophet could do carried with it an implied reproach upon the inability of the prophets of the

Syrian god Rimmon. On a similar score Naaman presently took offence at Elisha's directions: "Are not Abana and Pharpar, rivers of Damascus, better than all the waters of Israel?" (2 Kings 5:12). The little maid, then, was running the grave risk of "shame for His name". Whether this occurred to her or not we do not know. Maybe in the simplicity and warmth of her heart that never crossed her mind. We often raise difficulties that never materialize. In any case she bears her testimony and in an instant the good news is taken up and relayed to Naaman and the king himself and all Damascus is presently in a stir. Such far-reaching effects can one simple word of testimony have. "There shall be a handful of corn in the earth upon the top of the mountains: the fruit thereof shall shake like Lebanon" (Ps. 72:16). This then was the testimony that was instrumental in bringing health of body, and we would fain believe health of soul, to Naaman—a double cure.

(3) A happy outcome

One part of the story is hidden from us—the little maid's reaction on Naaman's return in health to his own home. There must have been undisguised joy in seeing her master made whole, like herself, and what utter satisfaction in having her faith in the God of Israel vindicated. Nor could she fail to discover something of the secret of that strange and apparently cruel providence that had brought her to Damascus. Like another captive she was honoured in being sent before "to save life by a great deliverance" (Gen. 45:7).

Is it beyond likelihood that the great man condescended to take notice of the little maid as never before. She had a special claim on his attention, for he owed to her, under God, his health and his salvation. Did they speak often one to another after this and think upon His Name? We have something of a New Testament parallel to encourage such a pleasing conception—it is that of Philemon and the converted slave, Onesimus. The runaway is sent back to his master but in wholly altered circumstances—"not now as a servant, but above a servant, a brother beloved, specially to me but how much more unto thee, both in the flesh and in the Lord" (Philem. 16).

We could have wished that the sequel to that raid had been communicated to the little maid's parents and that they had known how fruitful their early instruction had proved. Could they have heard the familiar truths they had imparted to their child no longer repeated by rote but come fresh and living from her heart to guide another into the way of peace, they would have "rejoiced with joy unspeakable". This is not to say but that, in the absence of such satisfaction, they went steadfastly on to live and die in faith, believing that in the service of such a faithful Master as theirs, their labour could never be "in vain in the Lord".

G. DUNNETT